IRACEMA

Contents

OXFORD

UNIVERSITY PRESS

Oxford New York
Athens Auckland Bangkok Bogotá
Buenos Aires Calcutta Cape Town Chennai Dar es Salaam
Delhi Florence Hong Kong Istanbul Karachi
Kuala Lumpur Madrid Melbourne
Mexico City Mumbai Nairobi Paris São Paolo Singapore
Taipei Tokyo Toronto Warsaw
and associated companies in
Berlin Ibadan

Copyright © 2000 by Oxford University Press, Inc.

Published by Oxford University Press, Inc.
198 Madison Avenue, New York, New York 10016

Oxford is a registered trademark of Oxford University Press, Inc.

Library of Congress Cataloging-in-Publication Data
Alencar, José Martiniano de, 1829–1877.
[Iracema. English]
Iracema : a novel / by José de Alencar ;
translated from the Portuguese by Clifford E. Landers ;
with a foreword by Naomi Lindstrom ;
and an afterword by Alcides Villaça.
p. cm.
ISBN 0-19-511547-3
ISBN 0-19-511548-1 (pbk.)
ISBN 13: 978-0-19-511548-2
1. Landers, Clifford E.
II. Title.
PQ9697.A53I813   2000
869.3—dc21   99-045927

Printed in the United States of America
on acid-free paper

IRACEMA

A Novel by
JOSÉ DE ALENCAR

Translated from the Portuguese by
CLIFFORD E. LANDERS

WITH A FOREWORD BY NAOMI LINDSTROM
AND AN AFTERWORD BY ALCIDES VILLAÇA

OXFORD
UNIVERSITY PRESS

Series Editors'
General Introduction

The Library of Latin America series makes available in translation major nineteenth-century authors whose work has been neglected in the English-speaking world. The titles for the translations from the Spanish and Portuguese were suggested by an editorial committee that included Jean Franco (general editor responsible for works in Spanish), Richard Graham (series editor responsible for works in Portuguese), Tulio Halperín Donghi (at the University of California, Berkeley), Iván Jaksić (at the University of Notre Dame), Naomi Lindstrom (at the University of Texas at Austin), Francine Masiello (at the University of California, Berkeley), and Eduardo Lozano of the Library at the University of Pittsburgh. The late Antonio Cornejo Polar of the University of California, Berkeley, was also one of the founding members of the committee. The translations have been funded thanks to the generosity of the Lampadia Foundation and the Andrew W. Mellon Foundation.

During the period of national formation between 1810 and into the early years of the twentieth century, the new nations of Latin America fashioned their identities, drew up constitutions, engaged in bitter struggles over territory, and debated questions of education, government, ethnicity, and culture. This was a unique period unlike the process of nation formation in Europe and one which should be more familiar than it is to students of comparative politics, history, and literature.

The image of the nation was envisioned by the lettered classes—a minority in countries in which indigenous, mestizo, black, or mulatto peasants and slaves predominated—although there were also alternative nationalisms at the grassroots level. The cultural elite were well educated in European thought and letters, but as statesmen, journalists, poets, and academics, they confronted the problem of the racial and linguistic heterogeneity of the continent and the difficulties of integrating the population into a modern nation-state. Some of the writers whose works will be translated in the Library of Latin America series played leading roles in politics. Fray Servando Teresa de Mier, a friar who translated Rousseau's *The Social Contract* and was one of the most colorful characters of the independence period, was faced with imprisonment and expulsion from Mexico for his heterodox beliefs; on his return, after independence, he was elected to the congress. Domingo Faustino Sarmiento, exiled from his native Argentina under the presidency of Rosas, wrote *Facundo: Civilización y barbarie,* a stinging denunciation of that government. He returned after Rosas' overthrow and was elected president in 1868. Andrés Bello was born in Venezuela, lived in London where he published poetry during the independence period, settled in Chile where he founded the University, wrote his grammar of the Spanish language, and drew up the country's legal code.

These post-independence intelligentsia were not simply dreaming castles in the air, but vitally contributed to the founding of nations and the shaping of culture. The advantage of hindsight may make us aware of problems they themselves did not foresee, but this should not affect our assessment of their truly astonishing energies and achievements. It is still surprising that the writing of Andrés Bello, who contributed fundamental works to so many different fields, has never been translated into English. Although there is a recent translation of Sarmiento's celebrated *Facundo,* there is no translation of his memoirs, *Recuerdos de provincia (Provincial Recollections).* The predominance of memoirs in the Library of Latin

America series is no accident—many of these offer entertaining insights into a vast and complex continent.

Nor have we neglected the novel. The series includes new translations of the outstanding Brazilian writer Joaquim Maria Machado de Assis' work, including *Dom Casmurro* and *The Posthumous Memoirs of Brás Cubas*. There is no reason why other novels and writers who are not so well known outside Latin America—the Peruvian novelist Clorinda Matto de Turner's *Aves sin nido*, Nataniel Aguirre's *Juan de la Rosa*, José de Alencar's *Iracema*, Juana Manuela Gorriti's short stories — should not be read with as much interest as the political novels of Anthony Trollope.

A series on nineteenth-century Latin America cannot, however, be limited to literary genres such as the novel, the poem, and the short story. The literature of independent Latin America was eclectic and strongly influenced by the periodical press newly liberated from scrutiny by colonial authorities and the Inquisition. Newspapers were miscellanies of fiction, essays, poems, and translations from all manners of European writing. The novels written on the eve of Mexican Independence by José Joaquín Fernández de Lizardi included disquisitions on secular education and law, and denunciations of the evils of gaming and idleness. Other works, such as a well-known poem by Andrés Bello, "Ode to Tropical Agriculture," and novels such as *Amalia* by José Mármol and the Bolivian Nataniel Aguirre's *Juan de la Rosa*, were openly partisan. By the end of the century, sophisticated scholars were beginning to address the history of their countries, as did João Capistrano de Abreu in his *Capítulos de história colonial*.

It is often in memoirs such as those by Fray Servando Teresa de Mier or Sarmiento that we find the descriptions of everyday life that in Europe were incorporated into the realist novel. Latin American literature at this time was seen largely as a pedagogical tool, a "light" alternative to speeches, sermons, and philosophical tracts—though, in fact, especially in the early part of the century, even the readership for novels was quite small because of the high rate of illiteracy. Nevertheless, the vigorous orally transmitted culture of the gaucho and the urban underclasses became the linguistic repertoire of some of the most interesting nineteenth-century writers—most notably José Hernández, author of the "gauchesque" poem "Martín Fierro," which enjoyed an unparalleled popularity. But for many writers the task was not to appropriate popular language but to civilize, and their literary works were strongly influenced by the high style of political oratory.

The editorial committee has not attempted to limit its selection to the better-known writers such as Machado de Assis; it has also selected many works that have never appeared in translation or writers whose work has not been translated recently. The series now makes these works available to the English-speaking public.

Because of the preferences of funding organizations, the series initially focuses on writing from Brazil, the Southern Cone, the Andean region, and Mexico. Each of our editions will have an introduction that places the work in its appropriate context and includes explanatory notes.

We owe special thanks to Robert Glynn of the Lampadia Foundation, whose initiative gave the project a jump start, and to Richard Ekman of the Andrew W. Mellon Foundation, which also generously supported the project. We also thank the Rockefeller Foundation for funding the 1996 symposium "Culture and Nation in Iberoamerica," organized by the editorial board of the Library of Latin America. We received substantial institutional support and personal encouragement from the Institute of Latin American Studies of the University of Texas at Austin. The support of Edward Barry of Oxford University Press has been crucial, as has the advice and help of Ellen Chodosh of Oxford University Press. The first volumes of the series were published after the untimely death, on July 3, 1997, of Maria C. Bulle, who, as an associate of the Lampadia Foundation, supported the idea from its beginning.

—*Jean Franco*
—*Richard Graham*

Foreword

José Martiniano de Alencar (1829–1877) was born in Mecejana, in the Brazilian state of Ceará, the region that serves as the setting for his 1865 novel *Iracema*. Best known as a novelist, Alencar also composed biographies, works for the theater, political analyses and polemics, meditative journalism, scholarly works, and writings in which he justified his literary and cultural positions and responded to his critics.

Alencar pursued a career in public affairs as well. He occupied the post of Minister of Justice from 1868 to 1870. Aspiring to a senate seat, he received the highest number of votes in the 1869 election, but the Emperor Pedro II, who had been the object of direct criticism from the novelist, did not approve of him for the position. Exercising his constitutional privilege, the Emperor appointed another of the top three finalists. Though his political career met with mixed success, by all accounts Alencar was one of the memorable orators of his day.

This preface concentrates on Alencar's activities that have bearing on the romantic, Indian-theme nationalism that *Iracema* embodies. It should be noted that, even within the single genre of the novel, Alencar covered a wide scope of themes and of geographical and historical settings. As a writer dedicated to creating Brazilian literature, he appears to have aimed, in his prose fiction, to touch upon every important aspect of the nation. In a notable omission, which Roberto Reis points out, "Blacks do not appear in Alencar's novels."[1]

Iracema is the second in Alencar's cycle of three Indianist novels: *O Guarani* (1857), *Iracema* (1865), and *Ubirajara* (1874). In addition, in 1863 Alencar began to compose a thematically related epic poem, "Os filhos de Tupã" (*The children of Tupã*). (This project remained unfinished, but was published posthumously in 1910 and 1911 in its fragmentary form.) A reader of these works glimpses behind them a complete program of ideas concerning the making of Brazilian literature. Alencar was, indeed, an author with an agenda. In his Indianist novels, he sought to create allegories of the genesis of the Brazilian people. Indian tribes particular to Brazil were useful in illustrating the uniqueness of national history. Stories of the encounters between Indians and early Portuguese settlers were also transformed into mythic narratives of a past shared by all Brazilians. This is especially true in *O Guarani* and *Iracema*; both novels deal not only with the early encounters, but also the profound changes this contact brings to indigenous peoples. *Ubirajara*, Alencar's third Indianist novel, is set in an earlier era. In it, Indians enjoy a changelessly beautiful primeval land before the arrival of the Europeans and the beginning of the nation's history.

The novelistic construction of *Iracema* depends on a flashback. The first chapter depicts a scene set after Iracema has already died. A bereaved European soldier is sailing away from Ceará. The opening does not explain why the protagonist is grieving and why he is sailing the ocean accompanied only by a small child and a dog. However, the narrator claims to possess an insider's knowledge of what is behind this curious scene. It is a local legend of Ceará, "a story that I was told in the beautiful plains where I was born."

After this first chapter, the narrator takes the reader through a lengthy retrospective. Chapters II through XXXII relate the events from Iracema's meeting with Martim through her death. The thirty-third chapter, resembling an epilogue, takes place four years after the events related in the rest of the novel. The protagonist and his child return from the journey to Portugal that they were seen undertaking in the first chapter. Martim sets to work strengthening Christianity, Indian-European relations, and Portuguese rule in Brazil, and the legend and the novel *Iracema* draw to a close.

Reading *Iracema*, North American readers will be reminded of the way that narratives of Pilgrims and Indians, and especially the story of the first Thanksgiving, have been elaborated to give the diverse U.S. population the sense of possessing a common past. In many respects, *Iracema* embodies the same general type of project underlying the Indian-theme novels of James Fenimore Cooper (1789–1851). Cooper, another writer determined to craft a national literature, felt a similar attraction to the era in which Indians and settlers first came into contact. Indeed, one of the criticisms leveled at *Iracema* when it was first published was that its author was imitating Cooper.

In focusing attention on the Indian component of the nation's heritage, Alencar was developing a tendency that arose during Brazil's push for Independence (1808–1822). Throughout Latin America, advocates and celebrators of Independence had idealized the Indian, not only as a being unique to the New World, but also as a figure of resistance to colonial rule. The sentimental glorification of native peoples was popularized during the Independence period and fit smoothly into the romanticism that came into fashion during the nineteenth century.

The principles and practices of Indianism in Brazilian literature were the topic of heated public discussion. Before any of his Indianist novels had appeared in print, Alencar was already a prime mover of this debate. In his 1856 comments on an Indianist poem by Domingos Gonçalves de Magalhães, Alencar seized the opportunity to set out his ideas on the topic. His remarks involved many of the nation's literary figures, as well as the Emperor, in a heated discussion of the themes of nationalism, Indianism, and romanticism. This interchange began the first of the great polemics on similar topics into which the author would be drawn.[2] As Alencar's own Indianist prose writings appeared, they in turn drew criticism. Using the passionate rhetoric typical of the romantic era, with its literary diatribes and polemics, Alencar defended his literary program and language. Unable to let his creative work speak for itself, Alencar composed numerous prefaces and afterwords to his novels as well as open letters and statements of his literary credo. His compulsive self-justification produced an extensive body of writing that affords readers a glimpse of the tempestuous literary world of mid- to late-nineteenth-century Brazil.

Alencar's campaign to create a Brazilian literary language was probably his most important contribution as a writer. In his search for elements that could generate a distinctive identity for Brazilian literature, Alencar studied the evolution of the Portuguese language as it was used in Brazilian life. Like many intellectuals of the romantic era, Alencar became a scholar of the orally transmitted folk narratives and beliefs and linguistic phenomena distinctive to his country, believing that the speech, sayings, and legends of the people could lead to a national identity. In his vision, the people included most specifically Brazil's indigenous communities. Among the many works the prolific Alencar produced is a lexical guide to the *Língua Brasílica*.

Alencar's struggle to forge a Brazilian expression is the basis for the respect he has enjoyed even after his romantic style went out of vogue. His efforts to write a more distinctively Brazilian literary language, however, drew heavy fire during the author's lifetime. The reaction of linguistic purists to Alencar's innovations was so virulent that it left the author embittered. At the same time, Alencar had influential contemporary supporters. The most distinguished of these was Joaquim Maria Machado de Assis, who would succeed Alencar as the nation's foremost literary figure. Alencar's struggle toward a Brazilian literary language appears to have also sparked the interest of the avant-gardist Mário de Andrade. Andrade's celebrated novel of 1928, *Macunaíma, O Herói Sem Nenhum Caráter*, mimics the Indianist discourse that Alencar had developed most clearly in his *Iracema*.[3]

Readers of *Iracema* will find, at the novel's end, Alencar's own statement of his ideas about the making of a Brazilian literary expression. As an afterword to the first edition, he included a letter addressed to his friend Domingos José Nogueira Jaguaribe (1820–1890). Alencar criticizes the use Brazilian romantics had been making of Indian characters, noting in particular their failure to draw upon the resources of the Indian language they have most closely at hand, Tupi. His ideal is the creation of a Brazilian literary medium that would derive full benefit from the author's knowledge of the Indian tongue. Literary borrowing from Indian language would be highly stylized, with esthetic considerations overruling the desire to be faithful to the actual speech of Indians. Alencar hoped to see "realized in it my ideas concerning national literature; and in it there will be an entirely Brazilian poetry, imbibed in the language of the savages." The ideas contained in the "Letter" continue to be of concern for

Brazilian literature. The struggle for a distinctive national identity, whether in the novel or in culture generally, remains a perennial problem.

Not all twentieth-century interest in Alencar has focused on his linguistic innovations, however. His Indianism has never been completely relegated to a bygone age of romanticism. Gilberto Freyre published a sympathetic book-length study of Alencar in 1955. Freyre, who made his name theorizing about racial and cultural identity in Brazil, brings his own central concerns to his reading of Alencar. He appreciates Alencar's focus on Indians as a salutary move away from the "Aryanist" outlook that Freyre associates with an ideal of whiteness, traditional Catholicism, denial of Brazil's diversity, and rigidly conventional bourgeois decorum. According to Freyre, by drawing attention to non-European elements in the making of the nation, Alencar becomes a more suitable Brazilian national writer than Machado de Assis, whom Freyre regarded as a hopeless Eurocentric.[4]

The novel *Iracema* is the story of a doomed amorous relationship between a beautiful young Tabajara Indian woman, Iracema, who is the daughter of a shaman, and a Portuguese soldier named Martim. Following romantic convention, the plot sets several obstacles in the way of their love. Martim is viewed as a menace by many members of the Tabajara tribe, who, according to Alencar's historical preface, were hostile to the Portuguese. Iracema's undisguised interest in Martim arouses the jealousy and enmity of "the great chieftain of the Tabajara nation," the hot-headed, treacherous Irapuã. As a priestess who officiates in Tabajara rituals, Iracema is a sacred virgin who is under vows of chastity. Her elopement with Martim outrages the Tabajaras and makes Iracema an outcast from her family and tribe.

In an additional complication, Iracema is more strongly attached to Martim than he is to her. Martim's inability to maintain his interest in Iracema soon sends her into a fatal decline from unrequited love. Ill-starred as their relation is, it succeeds in producing an heir of essential significance for the nation's future.

While the story of Iracema and Martim is the central plot, the relations that Martim establishes with both military and religious tribal leaders provide added complexities. Before his encounter with the inland Tabajaras— that is, before the events related in *Iracema*—Martim has already developed excellent relations with their longtime enemies, the Pitiguaras, a coastal tribe favorably disposed to the Portuguese. The Pitiguara chief Poti has become his spiritual brother. While on Tabajara lands, as an intruder and a friend of enemies, Martim is in danger of being killed by the tribe's leader and his men. Initially, he enjoys some protection from Iracema's family, a shamanistic household more concerned with ritual and symbolic matters than with intertribal politics and territorial defense. Though the chivalrous Martim struggles to behave with gentlemanly honor toward the Tabajaras, he ends up harming them. He finds that he has defiled the sacred virgin and is stealing her from her people. Though the shaman never forgives his daughter's defection, Iracema's brother Caubi is unusually sympathetic to her difficult situation.

The narrative is also an allegory for the genesis of Brazilian national culture. Probably many readers have noticed, as did the critic Afrânio Peixoto, that the heroine's name is an anagram of America.[5] Iracema at the outset is a priestess who enjoys a privileged rapport with nature and has supernatural abilities. She entrances Martim with a potion from a sacred tree. Later, her love for the European and consequent isolation from her tribe and homeland place her at a disadvantage and sap her powers. In this way, the Indian protagonist appears weaker as the novel's plot progresses. Though she remains captivated by Martim and cannot live without him, he can function without her. It is likely that many of today's women, coming to the end of the novel, have been disappointed at the dependency and weakness the heroine reveals in the final episodes.

If Iracema is America, then Martim is the European military man who takes over that land. Martim is the most civilized, sensitive, and gentlemanly of conquerors; explaining his personal code of honor, he differentiates sharply between his behavior on and off the battlefield. He does not wish to ill-repay his Tabajara host by deflowering the man's daughter and so defiling a sacred entity. Only while in a drug-induced trance does he give in to Iracema. Later, he is horrified to learn what he has done. As the hero of a nationalistic narrative, Martim frequently exhibits a desire to know and understand the land and to acquire distinctively Brazilian traits, including mastery of an indigenous language. Though the dialogue in the novel is rendered in a stylized Brazilian Portuguese with a few indigenous words, it is assumed that the characters are using an Indian tongue in which Martim is perfectly fluent. This character shares his author's concern with the folkways and beliefs of the native communities with whom he comes into contact. However, he stops considerably short of cultural relativism. For example, he wants to learn about tribal rituals, but also to supplant native religions with Christianity. In the final chapter, he brings to Brazil a priest "to plant the cross in the savage land" and baptize Martim's Brazilian "brother" Poti.

In the last chapter, the narrator draws attention to the significance of Moacir, the mestizo child of the union of Iracema and Martim. He refers to Moacir as "the first child born in Ceará"—although, of course, the area has long been inhabited by native peoples. Alencar, who was not shy about displaying the symbolic value of his Indianist narratives, suggests that the fate of this child foreshadows that of a just-emerging new people: "Did this presage the destiny of a race?" The reference to Moacir as the first citizen of Ceará—by extension, the first Brazilian—carries the implication that the Indians of precolonial times, while they were dwellers on the land, were not participants in regional or national history. In the vision projected in *Iracema*, native communities appear to have lived in the wild, enjoying a timeless unity with the natural world. The arrival of the Portuguese brings changes in this hitherto unblemished society, sets national history in motion, and marks the beginning of the Brazilian people.

The appearance of Moacir brings to the fore some of the novel's assumptions about race and nation. The Indian mother is able to conceive and bear the hybrid child; indeed, she skillfully gives birth without assistance. However, once born, Moacir cannot be sustained exclusively by his Indian mother. The languishing Iracema is unable to produce enough milk to nourish her baby. This circumstance suggests that the nation's Indian past, though poetic, is insufficient to allow it to grow strong and progress once the Portuguese arrive. Moacir appears to thrive, however, once Martim has taken over his care. Iracema carries out her function by transmitting the Indian heritage to her son. Yet this purely Indian heroine cannot live on into the new era, which will bring historical change.

By the time he collects his mestizo son, Martim is not quite as European as he was when he first met Iracema. The novel shows him accommodating himself to Brazil and its native communities. Throughout the novel, Martim's bond with his spiritual brother Poti grows steadily stronger, and with it his attachment to the new land. In part this interracial and intercultural brotherhood is forged naturally through their experiences together. But Martim and Poti also deliberately and symbolically affirm their connection and share attributes. For example, Poti gives Martim his faithful, beloved dog to maintain contact between them: "he will be the swift foot by which from far away we each run to the other" (Ch. XIX). Martim and Poti embrace as the former declares "The white warrior desires no other homeland but that of his son and of his heart" (Ch. XXIII). Most important in this series of interchanges are the two chapters (XXIV and XXXIII) that feature Martim and Poti in ceremonies that bring each into the other's culture.

Chapter XXIV stresses that Martim has "adopted the homeland of his wife and his friend." He becomes a member and warrior of the Pitiguara tribe, in which Poti serves as chief. The narrator shows him undergoing a body-painting ritual that will allow him "to become a red warrior, son of Tupā." The last phrase might seem to suggest that Martim is being initiated into the native religion and recognizing the divinity of Tupā. Nonetheless, the novel's closing chapter reveals Martim to be exclusively Christian, and so suggests that the earlier ceremony conferred only an honorary tribal membership. In this final chapter, the newly-baptized Poti is convinced that he and Martim "must have a single god." Further banishing any relativism in religious beliefs, the narrator refers to Christianity taking hold in Brazil: "The word of the true God germinated in the savage land." As the novel ends, it is unclear how far Martim has been willing to go in modifying his identity and outlook; the most far-reaching changes are clearly in store for the Indians.

Iracema is in many ways an exotic creature, especially when the narrator portrays her as the keeper of ancient tribal rites and admires her fleetness of foot in the thick woods. Even so, readers accustomed to nineteenth-century novels will notice that the Indian maiden shares many characteristics with the stylized heroines of romantic fiction. An example is the emphasis on Iracema's abundant and lengthy hair; the narrator exhibits the contemporary fascination with woman's hair as her crowning glory. Iracema has glowing, expressive eyes and an exceptionally sweet face. Her emotions are constantly on display. She sighs and turns pale when troubled; her face grows red with shame; she trembles and verges upon collapse; her face radiates light when she is happy.

She also has a number of more general attributes conventionally assigned to romantic heroines, such as youth and guileless impetuosity. Although Iracema drugs and seduces Martim (Chapter XV), she does not lose her purity of heart. The narrator continues to refer to her as "the maiden" after the seduction scene. This habit, at first confusing, is a way of ascribing to her some essential innocence that transcends material circumstances. Iracema is blinded by passion and makes unwise sacrifices for love. As the narrator points out when she abandons her family, priestess role, tribe, and lands: "The maiden's heart, like the warrior's, was deaf to the voice of prudence" (Chapter XVII). She refers to herself as enslaved by her love; she tells Martim "Master of Iracema, hear the plea of your slave" and impulsively offers to kill her own brother for his sake (Chapter XVIII). Finally, she dies a quintessentially romantic death from unrequited love.

Critical judgments of *Iracema* have fluctuated widely. Yet despite the range of opinions, the novel's critical reputation is substantially higher than when it was originally published. Alencar's first Indianist novel, *O Guarani*, enjoyed wide success with the reading public when it was serialized in the *Diário do Rio de Janeiro*. Aficionados of the serial reportedly gathered under streetlights to share the latest installment as soon as it appeared.[6] Popular enthusiasm was so strong that it may actually have damaged Alencar's standing with literary critics.

Iracema was not well received upon its publication. Machado de Assis, writing in January 1866 in the *Diário do Rio de Janeiro*, noted the scant attention accorded the novel. He sensed that dismissive contemporary judgments were not the last word on this innovative narrative. "*Iracema* must live as a work for the future," He wrote, "and we have faith that it will be read and appreciated, even when many of the works that are today in vogue are only cited in the bibliographic notes of some patient antiquarian."[7] Machado was correct. Of Alencar's many works, *Iracema* remains the one most regularly assigned to students at all levels. There have been two English translations of the book over the years prior to the present one, and it has also been translated into Spanish, French, and Latin.[8] The title of the novel has achieved symbolic significance as well. In 1975 the directorial team of Orlando Senna, Jorge Bodansky, and Wolf Gauer presented a film entitled *Iracema*. While their *Iracema* is an unromantic semi-documentary and not a dramatization of the plot of Alencar's celebrated work of fiction, it treats the impact on Brazilian Indians of outsiders' incursions into their land. The use of *Iracema* as a title demonstrates how Alencar's novel has marked the entire issue of Indian-white relations.

Today *Iracema* is securely established as a classic of Brazilian literature, but it is not purely a museum piece; it possesses relevance for the present day. The novel in some ways belongs completely to the nineteenth century, which from the perspective of today's insecure relativists seems marked by certainty. For example, few if any living literary intellectuals would exhibit Alencar's conviction that the conversion of Indians to Christianity was an absolute good. On the other hand, *Iracema* deals with issues that are still of vivid interest. The use of myth, allegory, and symbol to achieve a sense of national identity has in no way diminished since Alencar's time. Alencar's effort to create a Brazilian literary expression is an inextricable part of the development of the nation's literature. The manifestations of nationalism and the construction of national identity never cease to be of interest, and the same should hold true for *Iracema*.

—Naomi Lindstrom

NOTES

1. Roberto Reis, "Brazil," in David William Foster, ed., *Handbook of Latin American Literature*, 2nd. ed. (New York: Garland, 1992), p. 102. It is a noteworthy omission, since slavery and its oft-advocated abolition were then attracting so much attention on the Brazilian intellectual scene. Reis observes that the topic of slavery nonetheless appears in metaphorical guise in Alencar's novels, with weaker characters becoming enslaved to stronger ones. As noted, Iracema calls herself Martim's slave in Chapter XVIII of the novel.

2. José de Alencar began his career as a polemicist when he published *Cartas sobre "A confederação dos tamoios"* in 1856 in Rio de Janeiro, using the pseudonym Ig. The author's involvement in polemics over nationalism, romanticism, and Indianism is well documented, since the attacks and counter-attacks appeared in major newspapers. Today one may see a selection of Alencar's side of these disputes in Raimundo de Menezes, ed., *Cartas e documentos de José de Alencar, no centenário do romance "Iracema"* (São Paulo: Conselho Estadual de Cultura, 1967). Documents of the 1856 polemic, which involved many participants, were collected and prefaced by José Aderaldo Castello in the volume *A polêmica sobre "A confederação dos tamoios"* (São Paulo: Conselho Estadual de Cultura, 1953). Both sides of Alencar's stormy 1875 exchange with Joaquim Nabuco appear in Afrânio Countinho, ed., *A polêmica Alencar-Nabuco* (Rio de Janeiro: Tempo Brasileiro, 1965).

3. Mário de Andrade's *Macunaíma, O Herói Sem Nenhum Caráter*, first published in São Paulo in 1928, is available in English as *Macunaíma*, translated by E. A. Goodland (New York: Random House, 1984). Composed in a playful, parodic manner, *Macunaíma* features an Indian who leaves the jungle to become part of modern São Paulo. Among the many intellectual and literary currents that *Macunaíma* subjects to mimicry and critical reexamination is the Indianism epitomized by Alencar's *Iracema*, with its borrowings from Indian language, myth, and folkways to impart a Brazilian character to novelistic language. Many readers judge, with some justice, that Andrade is parodying *Iracema* (among other satirical targets) in *Macunaíma*. Yet the avant-garde writer's relation to Alencar is not

unilaterally derisive, since Andrade recognizes the earlier au-
thor's struggle to develop a Brazilian literary expression by
mining indigenous culture. The continuities between *Iracema*
and *Macunaíma* have attracted the attention of scholars. Two
studies comparing Alencar's and Andrade's celebrated novels
are Regina Zilberman, "Myth and Brazilian Literature," in
Fernando Poyatos, ed., *Literary Anthropology: A New Interdisci-
plinary Approach to People, Signs, and Literature* (Amsterdam:
Benjamins, 1988), pp. 141–51, and Roberto Ventura, "Literature,
Anthropology, and Popular Culture in Brazil: From José de
Alencar to Darcy Ribeiro," *Komparatistische Hefte* (Bayreuth,
Germany) 11 (1985): 35–47.

4. Gilberto Freyre, *Reinterpretando José de Alencar* (Rio de
Janeiro: Ministério de Educação e Cultura, Serviço de Docu-
mentação, 1955).

5. Afrânio Peixoto in his *Noçoes de história da literatura
brasileira* (Rio de Janeiro: F. Alves, 1931), p. 163, notes that the
letters of Iracema's name may be rearranged to spell *America*.

6. This and other manifestations of the widespread craze for
O Guarani are reported by José Luiz Beraldo, "Ceci e Peri, um
romance no Japão," in his anthology of the author, *José de Alen-
car* (São Paulo: Abril, 1980), p. 5.

7. Joaquim Maria Machado de Assis, "*Iracema* de José de
Alencar," collected by Jean-Michel Masse in *Dispersos* (Rio de
Janeiro: Instituto Nacional do Livro, 1965), pp. 229–30. Machado's
comments on *Iracema* and its relatively poor critical reception ap-
peared on 23 January 1866 in the *Diário do Rio de Janeiro*.

8. The previous English versions are *Iracema, the Honey-
Lips: A Legend of Brazil*, trans. Isabel Burton (London: Bicker
and Son, 1886), reprinted in 1976 by H. Fertig of New York,
and the lesser-known *Iracema (A Legend of Ceará)*, trans. N.
Biddell (Rio de Janeiro: Impresa Inglesa, 1921). The Spanish
Iracema, translated by María Torres Frías, appeared in Buenos
Aires in 1944. *Iracema, roman brésilien*, translated by Philéas
Lebesgue, was published in 1928 by Librairie Gedalce of Paris
in a single volume with *Joanna et Joel*, by Xavier Marques. In
1950, a Latin translation of *Iracema*, carried out by Remigio
Fernandez and Helena Coelho de Sousa Castro, was brought
out by the Imprensa Oficial of Belém (Brazil).

Translator's Note

The greatest challenge in translating a mid-nineteenth century romantic classic like *Iracema* was the question of tone. To a contemporary audience Alencar's prose can seem florid, even purple. A balance had to be found between literalism, which would make the text all but unreadable to today's audiences, and an overzealous modernization that would vitiate the exoticism and richness of vocabulary of the original.

Where there are no common equivalents to native animals and plants, or where a literal translation would introduce erroneous associations—such as "parakeet" for *jandaia*—they have been left in the original, provided the context makes the meaning clear. In other cases, they were either rendered into English or an explanatory word or phrase was interpolated. For example, in Chapter XIII, "warriors who crept along the ground like toads" conveys more meaning than "crept along the ground like the *intanha*." Nevertheless, because of the decision to include Alencar's Notes in the present edition, it was necessary to leave many words—those for which he analyzes their etymology—in the original, even where they are unclear in context. Such words are italicized, and any vagueness can be resolved by referring to the author's notes that follow the novel. Animal and plant names sufficiently anglicized to appear in the Oxford English Dictionary, such as agouti and carapa, are treated as English words and are not italicized, despite their strangeness to many readers.

Because the present version is aimed at a readership at the dawn of the twenty-first century, the second-person pronoun has been translated as *you* rather than *thou/thee*, except in cases where the speaker is addressing inanimate objects. Similarly, the author's use of the historical present, which occurs frequently but not consistently throughout the text, has been translated uniformly into the past tense.

Certain phrases may seemingly strike a false note—a notable one is "bite the dust" in Chapter XIV, because of associations with countless western films. The fact that *morder o pó* existed and was used by Alencar justifies its inclusion here, however jarring to contemporary ears. The metaphor is an obvious one to describe a fallen foe and quite likely evolved independently in numerous cultures.

In the final draft, a balance was sought between what the translator deemed as excessive reliance on either the archaic or the hypermodern. Some constructions have been rendered so as to suggest, without slavishly imitating, Alencar's sometimes idiosyncratic syntax—always correct and grammatical but often far removed from the common parlance of his own time. The reader must be the ultimate judge of how successful the effort has been.

—Clifford E. Landers

IRACEMA

I

G reen, impetuous seas of my native land, where the
jandaia sings amid the carnauba fronds:

Green seas, that gleam with liquid emerald in the
rays of the rising sun, skirting alabaster beaches shaded
by coconut trees:

Be still, green seas, and softly caress the raging wave
so the intrepid boat may calmly float above the waters.

Where is the brave raft bound, rapidly leaving be-
hind the coast of Ceará,[1] with its great sail open to the
cool wind from the shore?

Where is it bound, like a white kingfisher seeking
the native cliff in the ocean's solitude?

Three beings breathe upon the fragile wood that
quickly sails out to sea.

A young warrior whose white skin is not colored by
the blood of the Americas, a child and a mastiff who
first glimpsed the light in the forest's cradle and play
like brothers, sons both of the same savage land.

The intermittent gusts of wind bring from the beach a vibrant echo that resounds amid the surge of the waves: "Iracema!"[2]

The warrior youth, leaning against the rigging, maintains his captive eyes on the fleeting shades of the land: from time to time his gaze, clouded by a tenuous tear, falls upon the *jirau*[3] where rest the two innocent creatures, companions of his misfortune.

At that moment, his lips wrest from his soul a bitter smile.

What had he left behind in the land of exile?

A story that I was told in the beautiful plains where I was born, at dead of night, when the moon was gliding through the heavens silvering the countryside and the breeze rustled in the palm groves.

The wind grows cooler.

The crooning of the waves accelerates. The boat tosses upon the surf and disappears on the horizon. The immensity of the seas unfolds: and the tempest curves, like the condor, its dark wings over the abyss.

May God convey thee to safety, brave and proud boat, among the turbulent waves, and bring thee to land in some friendly bay. May gentle zephyrs blow for thee, and for thee may calm weather dot with color stormless seas.

While thou sailest thus at the mercy of the wind, graceful craft, let longing, which accompanies thee but does not depart from the land, return to the white sands where it soars.

II

Far, very far from that mountain that still looms
blue on the horizon, was Iracema born.

Iracema, the maiden with lips of honey, whose hair (1)
was darker than the *graúna's*[1] wings and longer than
her torso, straight and slender as the palm.

The *jati's*[2] honeycomb was not as sweet as her
smile; nor did the vanilla sending forth its fragrance in
the forest match the perfume of her breath.

Swifter than the wild ema, the tawny maiden tra-
versed the interior and the woodlands of Ipu,[3] where
dwelled her warrior tribe, of the great Tabajara[4] nation.
Her graceful, naked feet, scarcely touching the ground,
merely smoothed the green plush that carpeted the
earth with the first rains.

One day, when the sun was at its height, she was
resting in a clearing in the forest. The shade of an oiti-
cica,[5] cooler than the dew of night, bathed her body.
The branches of the wild acacia scattered flowers on

her damp hair. Hidden in the foliage, the birds coaxed forth their singing.

Iracema came from her bath. The pearly drops of water still bedewed her like the sweet *mangaba* fruit that blushed on a rainy morn. As she rested, she fixed to the arrows of her bow the feathers of the *gará*,[6] and joined the forest thrush, perched on a nearby branch, in its rustic song.

The graceful *ará*,[7] her companion and friend, played at her side. At times it winged its way to the branches of the tree and from there called the maiden by name; at other times it rummaged about in the *uru*,[8] the woven straw basket where the savage carried her perfumes, the white threads of the *crautá*[9] plant, the needles made from the *juçara*[10] thorns with which she wove the lace, and the dyes with which she colored the cotton.

A suspicious sound interrupted the gentle harmony of the afternoon warmth. The maiden lifted her eyes, which the sun did not bedazzle; what she saw disturbed her.

Standing before her and contemplating her was a strange warrior, if warrior he was and not some evil spirit of the forest. On his cheeks was the white of the sands that border the sea, in his eyes the melancholy blue of deep waters. Unknown weapons and unknown cloths covered his body.

As quick as the glance was Iracema's gesture. The arrow set in the bow flew. Drops of blood welled on the stranger's face.

Suddenly, his agile hand dropped to the hilt of his sword, but then he smiled. The young warrior had learned his mother's religion, in which the woman is symbol of tenderness and love. His suffering was more in the soul than in the wound.

The feeling expressed in his eyes and face I do not know. But the maiden cast aside the bow and *uiraçaba*[11]

4

and ran toward the warrior, regretting the pain she had caused.

The hand that had so quickly wounded, even more rapidly and compassionately stanched the dripping blood. Then Iracema snapped the murderous arrow; she handed the shaft to the stranger, keeping the barbed point.[12]

The warrior spoke.

"Are you breaking with me the arrow of peace?"

"Who has taught you, white warrior, my brothers' tongue? From where have you come to these woods, which have never seen another warrior like you?"

"I come from far away, daughter of the forests. I come from lands that your brothers once possessed and which my own now have."

"Welcome be the stranger to the land of the Tabajaras, lords of the villages, and to the hut of Araquém, father of Iracema."

III

The foreigner followed the maiden through the forest.

When the sun was gliding above the crest of the hills, and the turtledove first began to coo from the depths of the forest, they came upon the great village; and beyond, perched on the cliff, in the shadow of high jujube trees, the pajé's hut.

The old man was smoking at the door, sitting on a mat of carnauba and meditating on the sacred rites of Tupã. The tenuous breath of the wind disentangled, like flecks of cotton, his long, sparse white hair. So still was he that he seemed to conceal his life in his hollow eyes and deep wrinkles.

The pajé discerned in the distance the two approaching shapes; he thought he saw the shadow of a solitary tree that spread along the valley.

When the travelers entered the dense shade of the wood, then his gaze, like that of the jaguar, accustomed to the dark, recognized Iracema and saw that she was followed by a young warrior from a strange race and far-off lands.

The Tabajara tribes from beyond the Ibiapaba[1] mountains spoke of a new race of warriors, white as tempest flowers, come from remote shores on the banks of the Mearim. The old man thought it was a such a warrior who now trod the native lands.

Calmly, he waited.

The maiden pointed to the foreigner and said, "Father, he has come."

"And well has he come. It is Tupã who brings the guest to Araquém's hut."

Saying this, the pajé handed his pipe to the foreigner, and they went into the hut.

The youth sat in the main hammock, which hung in the middle of the dwelling.

Iracema lit the fire of hospitality and brought what there were of provisions to satisfy hunger and thirst: she brought the rest of the hunt, the manioc meal, the wild fruits, the honeycombs, the cashew wine, and pineapples.

Then the maiden came in with a *igaçaba*[2] that she had filled with cool water at a nearby spring to wash the foreigner's face and hands.

When the warrior had finished the meal, the aged pajé extinguished the pipe and spoke: "Have you come?"[3]

"I have come," the stranger replied.

"You are welcome. The foreigner is lord of Araquém's hut. The Tabajaras have a thousand warriors to defend him and women beyond count to serve him. Speak, and all will obey you."

"Pajé, I thank you for the kind reception you have accorded me. As soon as the sun rises, I shall leave your hut and your lands to which, lost, I came; but I must not leave them without telling you who is the warrior whom you have befriended."

7

"It was Tupã whom the pajé has served; he brought you, he will take you from here. Araquém has done nothing for his guest; he asks not from where he comes or when he goes. If you wish to sleep, may happy dreams descend upon you; if you would talk, your host listens."

The foreigner said, "I am from the white warriors who built the village on the banks of the Jaguaribe,[4] near the sea, where the Pitiguaras,[5] the enemies of your nation, live. My name is Martim,[6] which in your language means son of a warrior; my blood, that of the great people who first saw the lands of your country. My vanquished comrades have returned by sea to the banks of the Paraíba, from whence they came, and their leader, forsaken by his own, is now crossing the vast interior of Apodi. From among so many, I alone remained, for I was among the Pitiguaras of Acaracu,[7] in the hut of brave Poti, brother of Jacaúna, who planted with me the tree of friendship. Three suns ago we left for the hunt, and, strayed from my own, I came to the land of the Tabajaras."

"It was some evil spirit of the forest[8] that blinded the white warrior in the darkness of the woods," replied the old man.

The *cauã* chirped in the far reaches of the valley. Night was falling.

IV

The pajé rattled the gourd and left the hut, but the foreigner was not alone.

Iracema had returned with the women summoned to serve Araquém's guest and the warriors come to obey him.

"White warrior," the maiden said, "may pleasure rock your hammock during the night, and the sun bring light to your eyes, happiness to your soul."

And as she said this, Iracema's lip trembled, and her eyelids were moist.

"Do you leave me?" Martim asked.

"The most beautiful women of the great village stay with you."[1]

"For them, Araquém's daughter should not have led the guest to the pajé's hut."

"Stranger, Iracema cannot be your servant. It is she who guards the secret of the *jurema*[2] and the mystery of dreams. Her hand makes for the pajé the drink of Tupã."

The Christian warrior crossed the hut and disappeared into the darkness.

The great village rose in the depths of the valley, illuminated by the torches of joy. The gourd rumbled; to the slowly changing tones of the wild chant, the dance throbbed to the crude rhythm. Inspired, the pajé led the sacred dance and told the believers of the secrets of Tupã.

The great chieftain of the Tabajara nation, Irapuã,[3] had descended from the heights of the Ibiapaba mountains to lead the tribes of the interior against the Pitiguara enemy. The warriors of the valley celebrated the coming of the chieftain and the next battle.

The Christian youth saw from afar the brightness of the feast; he continued and saw the blue, cloudless sky. The unmoving star[4] that shone above the forest canopy guided his firm steps toward the cool banks of the river of herons.

When he had crossed the valley and was about to enter the forest, Iracema's shadow appeared. The maiden had followed the foreigner like the subtle breeze that without rustling glides through the branches.

"Why," she said, "does the foreigner desert the hut of hospitality without taking the gift of return? Who in the land of the Tabajaras has done evil to the white warrior?"

The Christian saw how just was her complaint and thought himself ungrateful.

"No one did injury to your guest, daughter of Araquém. It was the desire to see his friends that took him away from the lands of the Tabajaras. He did not take the gift of return, but he takes in his soul the memory of Iracema."

"Were the memory of Iracema in the foreigner's soul, it would not let him depart. The wind does not take away the sand of the meadow when the sand drinks the water from the rain."

The maiden sighed.

"White warrior, stay until Caubi returns from the hunt. The brother of Iracema has the subtle ear that senses the *boicininga*[5] snake among the sounds of the woods, and the eye of the *oitibó*[6] that sees better in darkness. He will guide you to the banks of the river of herons."

"How much time will pass before Iracema's brother returns to Araquém's hut?"

"The sun, which is to be born, will return with the warrior Caubi to the lands of the Ipu."

"Your guest will wait, daughter of Araquém; but if the returning sun does not bring Iracema's brother, with it will go the white warrior to the village of the Pitiguaras."

Martim returned to the pajé's hut.

The white hammock, which Iracema had perfumed with aromatic resin of benjamin, awaited him with a sleep both calm and sweet.

The Christian fell asleep hearing the tender song of the Indian maiden sighing among the murmurs of the forest.

V

The black-throated cardinal lifted its scarlet tuft from the nest.

Its limpid trill announced the coming of day.

Shadow still covered the earth. The savage folk gathered their hammocks in the great village and walked toward their bath. The old pajé, who had spent the night without sleep, speaking to the stars, warding off the evil spirits of the darkness,[1] furtively entered the hut.

Once again the bamboo pipe, the *boré*,[2] resounded through the expanse of the valley.

The swift warriors took up their weapons and ran to the field. When all were in the *ocara*,[3] a vast circular meeting place, Irapuã, the chief, loosed the cry of war:

"Tupã has given to the great Tabajara nation all this land. We protect the mountains, from which flow the streams, with the cool and fertile places where the cassava and cotton grow; and we abandoned to the bar-

barous Potiguara,[4] eaters of shrimp, the naked sands of the sea, with their dry plains with neither water nor forest. Now the fishers of the beach, forever beaten, allow the white race of warriors of fire, the enemies of Tupã, to come by sea. The *emboabas* have already been to the Jaguaribe; soon they will be in our lands, and with them the Potiguaras. Shall we, lords of the villages, do as the dove, which shrinks into its nest when the serpent coils around the branches?"

The angry chieftain brandished his club and hurled it into the middle of the circle. Lowering his head, he concealed his wrathful gaze. "Irapuã has spoken," he said.

The youngest of the warriors came forward:

"The falcon hovers in the air. When the *nambu* takes to the air, the falcon drops from the clouds and rends its victim's entrails. The Tabajara warrior, son of the mountains, is like the falcon."

A *pocema*[5] of war sounded again and again.

The young warrior had raised his club and brandished it in turn. Spinning in the air, rapidly and menacingly, the chieftain's weapon passed from hand to hand.

Old Andira,[6] the pajé's brother, let it fall to the earth and stamped on the ground, his foot still agile and firm.

The Tabajara people were astonished at this strange act. A vow of peace from such a tested and furious warrior! Was this the aged hero, whose rage had grown in the same measure as his years, was it the ferocious Andira who dropped the club, harbinger of the next struggle?

Uncertain and wordless, everyone listened:

"Andira, old Andira, has drunk more blood in war than all the warriors who now give light to his eyes have drunk cashew wine in the feasts of Tupã. He has seen more battles in his life than the moons that left bare his scalp. How many Potiguara skulls had his merciless hand already scalped before time plucked from his head the first hair? And old Andira never feared that the enemy would walk the land of his fathers but rejoiced when he came, and at the scent of war felt youth being reborn in his enfeebled body as the dry tree is reborn with the breath of winter. The Tabajara nation is wise. It should lay aside the war club to play the flute of the feast. Celebrate, Irapuã, the arrival of the *emboabas* and let them all come to our lands. Then Andira promises you the banquet of victory."

Then Irapuã loosed his deep rage.

"You stay, hidden among the wine vessels; stay, old bat, because you fear the light of day and drink the blood only of the victim who sleeps. Irapuã carries war in the handle of his club. The terror that he inspires flies with the hoarse sound of the bamboo pipe. The Potiguara have already trembled, hearing it roar in the mountains, stronger than the thundering of the sea."

VI

Martim walked slowly between the tall jujube trees that encircled the pajé's hut.

It was the time when the mild *aracati*[1] comes from the sea and spreads its delightful cool breeze through the arid inland. The plants breathed; a gentle shiver bristled the forest's green mane.

The Christian contemplated the sunset. The shadow, descending from the hills and covering the valley, penetrated his spirit. He remembered the place where he was born, the loved ones he had left there. Could he know whether one day he would see them again?

Around him, nature lamented the dying of day. Timorous and tearful, the wave sobbed; the wind moaned in the branches, and silence itself pined in its oppression.

Iracema stopped before the young warrior.

"Is it Iracema's presence that disturbs the serenity on the foreigner's face?"

Martim rested his gentle eyes on the maiden's face.

"No, daughter of Araquém; your presence brings joy, like the morning light. It was the memory of my homeland that brought longing to my foreboding heart."

"Does a bride await you?"

The stranger averted his eyes. Iracema leaned her head on her shoulder, like the tender carnauba palm when the rain penetrates the tilled plains.

"She is not sweeter than Iracema, the maiden with lips of honey, nor more beautiful!" the foreigner murmured.

"The flower of the woods is beautiful when it has a limb to shelter it, a trunk around which to entwine. Iracema does not live in the soul of a warrior: never has she felt the cool of his smile."

They fell silent, their eyes downcast, hearing only the beating of their oppressed hearts.

The maiden spoke at last: "Happiness will soon return to the white warrior's soul, because Iracema wants him to see before the coming of night the bride that awaits him."

Martim smiled at the guileless desire of the pajé's daughter.

"Come!" said the maiden.

They crossed the woods and went down into the valley. Where the side of the mountain ended, the grove of trees was thick: a dense vault of dark-green foliage covered the sylvan sanctuary reserved for the mysteries of the barbaric rite.

These were the sacred *jurema* woods. Around them stood the gnarled trunks of Tupã's tree; from its limbs, hidden among the dark branches, hung the sacrificial urns. The ground was covered with the ashes of an extinguished fire, which had served the feast of the latest moon.

Before penetrating the secret site, the maiden, who was leading the warrior by the hand, hesitated, inclining her keen ear to the sighing of the wind. Each slight sound of the woods had its own voice for the savage daughter of the interior. But there was nothing suspicious in the intense breathing of the forest.

Iracema gestured to the foreigner to wait and be silent; she then quickly disappeared into the darkest part of the woods. The sun still hovered suspended in the heights of the mountain ridge, and deep night was filling that solitude.

When the maiden returned, she brought on a leaf drops of a strange green liquor poured from the vase that she had taken from the bosom of the earth. She handed the warrior the rustic cup:

"Drink!"

Martim felt the sleep of death pass before his eyes; but light quickly flooded the deepest reaches of his soul, and strength abounded in his heart. He relived past days better than he had first lived them; he enjoyed the reality of his most beautiful hopes.

Behold him returning to the land of his birth, embracing his aged mother, seeing again more lovely and tender the pure angel of his childhood loves.

But why, as soon as he returned to the cradle of his homeland, did the young warrior again leave the shelter of his country, and go in search of the interior?

He crossed the forests; he arrived at the lands of Ipu. He sought in the woods the pajé's daughter. He followed the coy maiden's delicate trail, releasing to the wind with frequent sighs the gentle name: "Iracema! Iracema!"

He overtook her and encircled her slender waist in his arms.

Yielding to the loving pressure, the maiden leaned against the warrior's chest, where she remained, trembling and pulsing like a timid partridge when its loving mate ruffles its soft down with its beak.

The warrior's lips breathed again that sweet name, and sobbed, as if he had called to him the lips of a lover. Iracema felt her soul escaping to melt into the ardent kiss.

His head leaned toward her, and the beauty of her smile opened like the water lily at the kiss of the sun.

Suddenly the maiden trembled; swiftly freeing herself from the arms that encircled her, she picked up her bow.

VII

Iracema passed between the trees, silent as a shadow; her sparkling gaze filtered through the leaves like a tenuous beam of starlight; she listened to the deep silence of the night and breathed the delicate breezes that were stirring.[1]

She stopped. A shadow was gliding through the foliage; and the leaves crackled to a light footstep, if not the gnawing of some insect.

Little by little, the slight sound grew, and the shadow took on form.

It was a warrior. With a leap, the maiden was facing him, tremorous from fright but even more from anger.

"Iracema!" the warrior exclaimed, drawing back.

"Anhangá[2] surely disturbed Irapuã's sleep, for him to become lost in the *jurema* woods, where no warrior penetrates against Araquém's will."

"It was not Anhangá, but the memory of Iracema, that disturbed the sleep of the first among the Tabajara warriors. Irapuã descended from his eagle's aerie to follow in the plains the river heron. He arrived, and Iracema fled from his eyes. The voices in the villages spoke into the chieftain's ear that a foreigner had come to Araquém's hut."

The maiden shuddered. The warrior fixed his blazing gaze on her: "The heart here in Irapuã's chest became enraged. It leapt in wrath. It came pursuing the scent of its prey. The foreigner is in the woods, and Iracema was with him. I would drink all his blood; when the white warrior's blood runs in the Tabajara chieftain's veins, perhaps then Araquém's daughter will love him."

The maiden's dark eyes flashed in the night, and on her lips, like a drop of caustic sap from the spurge, welled a disdainful smile.

"Never would Iracema give her bosom, where none but the spirit of Tupã dwells, to the basest of the Tabajara warriors! Vile is the bat for it flees from the light and drinks the blood of its sleeping victim!"

"Daughter of Araquém, provoke not the jaguar! The name of Irapuã flies farther than the wild duck of the lake when it senses the rain beyond the mountains. Let the white warrior come, and let Iracema's heart open to the victor."

"The white warrior is the guest of Araquém. Peace brought him to the lands of Ipu, and it is peace that protects him. He who offends the foreigner, offends the pajé."

The Tabajara chieftain roared in fury: "Irapuã's wrath now hears only the cry of revenge. The foreigner will die."

"Araquém's daughter is stronger than the chieftain of the Tabajaras," said Iracema, seizing the war trumpet. "She holds the voice of Tupã, who calls his people."

"But he will not call!" replied the chieftain mockingly.

"No, because Irapuã will be punished by the hand of Iracema. His first step is the step of death."

The maiden sprang back from the forward position she had taken and brandished her bow. The chieftain was still gripping his formidable club, but for the first time he felt it weighing heavily on his powerful arm. The blow that would wound Iracema, though not struck, had already pierced his own heart.

He knew then how much is the strongest man, by his very strength, more the captive of great passions.

"The shadow of Iracema will not forever hide the foreigner from the vengeance of Irapuã. Vile is the warrior who accepts the protection of a woman."

Speaking these words, the chieftain disappeared among the trees. Ever alert, the maiden returned to the sleeping Christian, and watched at his side for the rest of the night. The emotions that so recently had shaken her soul had opened her even more to the gentle affection with which the foreigner's eyes were imbuing her.

She wished to shelter him against all danger, draw him unto her as in an impenetrable asylum. Following her thoughts, her arms embraced the warrior's head and hugged it to her breast.

But when the joy of seeing him safe from the dangers of the night had passed, the keenest disquietude made its way into her at the remembrance of the new dangers yet to come.

"Iracema's love is like the wind of the sandy ground; it kills the flowers of the trees," sighed the maiden.

And she walked slowly away.

VIII

The dawn opened the day and the white warrior's eyes. The morning light dissipated the night's dreams and tore from his soul the remembrance of what he had dreamed. There remained only a vague feeling, as in the copse there remains the perfume of the flower denuded in the morning by the mountain wind.

He did not know where he was.

Upon leaving the sacred wood, he found Iracema. The maiden was leaning against a rough tree trunk in the grove; her eyes were downcast, and the blood had fled from her cheeks. Her heart trembled on her lips, like a dewdrop on the bamboo leaves.

Neither smiles nor color had the Indian maiden; neither buds nor roses has the acacia that the sun has singed; neither blue nor stars has the night saddened by the winds.

"The flowers of the forest have opened to the rays of the sun; the birds have begun to sing," said the warrior. "Why does Iracema alone bow her head in silence?"

The pajé's daughter shuddered. It is thus that the green palm shudders when its fragile trunk is shaken; the spar is bedewed with the tears of the rain, and the flycatchers rustle softly.

"The warrior Caubi is going to arrive at the village of his brothers. The foreigner can leave with the rising sun."

"Iracema would see the foreigner outside the land of the Tabajaras; then happiness will return to her breast."

"The *juriti*, when the tree dies, flees the nest where it was born. Never again will happiness return to Iracema's breast; it will become like the naked trunk, with neither branches nor shade."

Martim shielded the maiden's trembling body; she leaned wearily against the warrior's chest, like the tender shoot of the vanilla plant that entwines the unyielding angico branch.

The youth murmured, "Your guest will stay, dark-eyed maiden. He will stay to see the flower of happiness open on your cheeks, and to sip, like the hummingbird, the honey of your lips."

Iracema freed herself from the youth's arms and looked at him sadly.

"White warrior, Iracema is the pajé's daughter and guards the secret of the *jurema* tree. The warrior who possessed the virgin of Tupã would die."

"And Iracema?"

"You would die . . ."

The word was like a troubled sigh. The youth's head fell and hung against his chest; but he quickly stood erect.

"The warriors of my blood bring death inside them, daughter of the Tabajaras. They fear it not for themselves, nor do they spare it to the enemy. But never, unless it be in combat, will they leave unsealed the maiden's *camucim*[1] in the village of her guest. Truth has spoken through Iracema's mouth. The foreigner must abandon the lands of the Tabajaras."

"He must," replied the maiden like an echo.

Then her voice sighed: "The honey of Iracema's lips is like the honeycomb that the bees make in the *andiroba*[2] trunk: there is poison in its sweetness. The blue-eyed maiden with hair the color of the sun[3] keeps for her warrior in the white man's village the honey of the white lily."

Martim walked quickly away; but he slowly returned. The words trembled on his lips: "The foreigner will leave so that peace can return to the maiden's bosom."

"You take with you the light of Iracema's eyes and the flower from her soul."

A strange clamor resounded in the forest. The youth's eyes widened.

"It is the cry of joy of the warrior Caubi," said the maiden. "The brother of Iracema announces that he has arrived at the lands of the Tabajara."

"Daughter of Araquém, guide your guest to the hut. It is time to go."

They walked side by side, like two young deer who at sunset cross the *capoeira*,[4] the second-growth land, withdrawing into the retreat from which the breeze brings a suspect scent.

When they drew near the jujubes, they saw the warrior Caubi ahead of them, carrying on his powerful shoulders the weight of the hunt. Iracema walked toward him.

The foreigner entered the hut alone.

IX

The sleep of morning still rested on the pajé's eyes like the fine-weather mist that hovers at daybreak over the deep caverns of the mountain.

Martim stopped, uncertain; but the sound of his steps penetrated the old one's ear and shook his frail body.

"Arequém sleeps!" murmured the warrior, stepping backward.

The old one remained motionless.

"The pajé sleeps because Tupã has turned his face toward the earth and the light has put to flight the evil spirits of darkness. But sleep is soft on Araquém's eyes, like the smoke of *sape* grass at the crest of the ridge. If the foreigner has come to the pajé, then speak: his ear will hear."

"The foreigner has come to tell you he is leaving."

"In Araquém's hut, the guest is master: all paths are open to him. May Tupã guide him to the village of his people."

Caubi and Iracema arrived.

"Caubi has returned," said the Tabajara warrior. "He brings to Araquém the best of his hunt."

"The warrior Caubi is a great hunter of hills and forest. His father's eyes are happy to see him."

The old man opened his eyelids and quickly closed them.

"Daughter of Araquém, choose for your guest a gift of departure and make ready the *moquém*[1] for his journey. If the foreigner needs a guide, the warrior Caubi, master of the pathway,[2] will go with him."

Sleep returned to the pajé's eyes.

As Caubi hung on the smoke-rack the quarry from the hunt, Iracema gathered her hammock of purest white cotton fringed with feathers and placed it in the straw basket.

Martim waited at the door of the hut. The maiden came to him:

"O warrior who takes with him the sleep of my eyes, take my hammock too. When you sleep in it, may dreams of Iracema speak in your soul."

"Your hammock, maiden of the Tabajaras, shall be my companion in the wilderness. Though come the cold wind of night, it will hold for the foreigner the warmth and perfume of Iracema's bosom."

Caubi left for his hut, which he had not yet seen since his return. Iracema went to prepare the meat for the journey. They were alone in the hut: the pajé, who was snoring, and the youth with his sorrow.

The sun, past its zenith, was beginning to set in the west when Iracema's brother returned from the great village.

"This will be a sad day,"[3] said Caubi. "The shadows walk toward the night. It is time to leave."

The maiden rested her hand lightly on the cord of Araquém's hammock.

"He is leaving!" she murmured with trembling lips.

The pajé rose in the middle of the hut and lit his pipe. He and the youth shared the smoke of leave-taking.

"Just as the guest was welcomed to the hut of Araquém, so too is he wished a good journey."

The old man went to the door, to release into the wind a thick cloud of tobacco. When the smoke had dissipated into the air, he murmured, "May Jurupari[4] hide to let the pajé's guest go his way."

Araquém returned to his hammock and once again went to sleep. The youth picked up the weapons that, upon arriving, he had hung from the poles of the hut, and made ready to leave.

Caubi proceeded onward; some distance after him, the foreigner; immediately behind, Iracema.

They descended the hill and entered the somber forest. The rusty-flanked thrush, the tender songbird of evening, hidden amid the dense thickets of *ubaia*,[5] was already beginning to pour forth the prelude to its soft threnody.

The maiden sighed: "The evening is the sadness of the sun. Iracema's days will be long evenings with no morning, until the great night comes for her."

The youth had turned around. His lips remained mute, but his eyes spoke. A tear ran down the warrior's cheek, like the dampness that in summer's heat exudes from rocky cliffs.

Heading ever onward, Caubi disappeared among the thick foliage.

The bosom of Araquém's daughter heaved like the cresting of a wave as, sobbing, it breaks into fringes of foam. But her soul, dark with melancholy, still bore a pale reflection to light the dry flower of her cheeks. It is thus that a will-o'-the-wisp on a dark night comes to glow amidst the white sands of the plains.

"Foreigner, take the last of Iracema's smiles . . . and go!"

The warrior's mouth touched the maiden's delicate mouth. They stood there united like twin fruits of the *araçá* emerged from the heart of a single flower.

The voice of Caubi beckoned the foreigner. Iracema, lest she fall, clung to the trunk of a palm.

X

In his silent hut, the pajé meditated. Iracema was leaning against the rough trunk, which served as support. Her large, dark eyes, staring at the clearings in the forest and hollow from crying, were in those long, tremulous gazes stringing and unstringing the seed pearls of tears that bedewed her cheeks.

The *jandaia*,[1] perched on the facing pallet, cast its sad green eyes upon its beautiful mistress. From the moment the white warrior had set foot on the land of the Tabajaras, Iracema had forgotten it.

The maiden's rosy lips had not opened again for it to pluck from between them the pulp of fruit or the green corn mush: nor had the gentle hand caressed it a single time, smoothing the golden down of its head.

If it repeated the sweet name of its mistress, Iracema's smile no longer turned toward it, nor did her ear seem to hear the voice of her friend and companion, who earlier had been so pleasing to her heart.

Poor creature! The Tupi people called it *jandaia* because, ever joyful, it made the fields resound happily with its vibrant song. But now, sad and mute, disdained by its mistress, it no longer seemed the pretty *jandaia* but the ugly goatsucker, which knows only how to moan.

The sun withdrew to the western side of the mountains; its rays gilded only the top of the peaks.

The melancholy stillness of afternoon, preceding the silence of the night, was beginning to veil the repeated sounds of the countryside. A nocturnal bird, perhaps deceived by the deeper shadow of the forest, began to shrill.

The old man raised his bald brow.

"Was it the *inhuma*'s[2] song that awoke Araquém's ear?" he said, surprised.

The maiden had trembled, and, already outside the hut, turned to answer the pajé's question: "It was the war cry of the warrior Caubi!"

When the second chirp of the *inhuma* resounded, Iracema was running through the forest, like the doe pursued by the hunter. She breathed again only when she arrived at the meadow, which separated the woods like a large lake.

Her eyes first saw Martim, sitting calmly on the root of a tree, watching what was happening there. Opposite him, one hundred Tabajara warriors, with Irapuã at their head, formed an arc. The brave Caubi faced them all, his gaze filled with wrath and his valiant weapons grasped in his powerful hand.

The chieftain had demanded that the foreigner be handed over, and his guide had replied simply, "Kill Caubi first."

The pajé's daughter had come forward like an arrow; behold her in front of Martim, also opposing her slender body to the warriors' blows. Irapuã roared like the jaguar attacked in its lair.

"Daughter of the pajé," said Caubi in a low voice, "take the foreigner to the hut; Araquém alone can save him."

Iracema turned to the white warrior: "Come!"

He remained immobile.

"If you do not come, " said the maiden, "Iracema will die with you."

Martim stood up; but, far from following the maiden, he went directly to Irapuã. His sword blazed in the air.

"The warriors of my race, O chief, have never refused combat. If the one you see before you was not the first to provoke it, it is because his father and mother taught him not to shed blood in the land where he is guest."

The Tabajara chieftain bellowed with joy; his mighty hand brandished the club. But the two champions scarcely had time to take each other's measure with their eyes; when they launched the first blow, Caubi and Iracema were already between them.

In vain, Araquém's daughter begged the Christian, in vain she wrapped her arms around him, trying to wrest him away from the fray. For his part, Caubi was futilely provoking Irapuã in order to attract to himself the chieftain's rage.

At a gesture from Irapuã, the warriors pulled the brother and sister aside; the combat proceeded.

Suddenly the hoarse sound of the war trumpet[3] reverberated through the forest; the sons of the mountain shuddered, recognizing the shrill sound of the battle conch shell of the Pitiguaras, lords of the beaches shaded by coconut palms. The echo came from the great village, which the enemy might already be attacking.

The warriors rushed away, their chieftain in the lead. With the foreigner remained only the daughter of Araquém.

XI

The Tabajara warriors, come in haste to the village, awaited the enemy before the stockade.

As he did not come, they went in search of him.

They scoured the surrounding woods and went through the fields; they found no sign of the Pitiguaras' passage; but the familiar roar of the conch shell from the shores had echoed in the mountain warriors' ears: there could be no doubt.

Irapuã suspected it was a trick by Araquém's daughter to save the foreigner, and he went directly to the pajé's hut. As the *guará*,[1] the wild dog, moves quickly along the edge of the woods, when following the spoor of its escaping prey, so did the enraged warrior quicken his pace.

Araquém, seeing the great chieftain of the Tabajara nation enter his hut, did not move. Seated in his hammock with his legs crossed, he was listening to Iracema. The maiden was relating the afternoon's events; upon seeing the sinister figure of Irapuã, she leapt to her bow and stood at the young warrior's side.

Gently, Martim separated himself from her and advanced.

The protection given him, a warrior, by the Tabajara maiden displeased him.

"Araquém, the vengeance of the Tabajaras awaits the white warrior; Irapuã has come for him."

"The guest is a friend of Tupã: whoever offends the foreigner will hear the thunder's roar."

"It was the foreigner who offended Tupã by stealing his maiden, who keeps the dreams of the *jurema*."

"Your mouth lies like the hiss of the *jobóia*,"[2] exclaimed Iracema.

Martim said, "Irapuã is base and unworthy of being the chieftain of valiant warriors!"

The pajé spoke slowly and gravely: "If the maiden abandoned to the white warrior the flower of her body, she will die; but the guest of Tupã is sacred. No one shall offend him; Araquém protects him."

Irapuã bellowed; the hoarse shout resounded in the cavity of his chest like the rumble of the *sucuri*[3] in the river's depths.

"The wrath of Irapuã no longer hears you, old pajé! Let it fall upon you, if you dare save the foreigner from the vengeance of the Tabajara."

Old Andira, the pajé's brother, entered the hut; in his hand was the terrible club, and in his eyes a fury more terrible still.

"The bat has come to suck your blood, Irapuã, if it is blood and not honey you have in your veins,[4] you who threaten the old pajé in his hut."

Araquém pushed his brother aside: "Peace and silence, Andira."

The pajé had unfolded his tall, thin body, like the rat snake when provoked, which rears up on its tail to face its victim. His wrinkles deepened, and drawing in his shriveled skin, his white, tapering teeth opened wide: "Dare one more step, and the wrath of Tupã will crush you under the weight of this gaunt and withered hand!"

"At this moment, Tupã is not with you!" replied the chieftain.

The pajé laughed, and his funereal laughter resounded through the dwelling like the snort of the river otter.

"Hear his thunder[5] and tremble in your soul, warrior, like the earth in its depths."

Proffering these terrible words, Araquém advanced to the middle of the hut; there he lifted the large stone and stamped his foot on the ground. Suddenly, the earth parted. From the deep cavern came a frightful moan that seemed to be torn from the rock's very entrails.

Irapuã did not tremble, nor faint from fright; but he felt the light quiver in his eyes and his voice on his lips.

"The lord of thunder is for you; the lord of war will be for Irapuã," said the chieftain.

The forbidding warrior left the hut; his large torso soon plunged into the shadows of twilight.

The pajé and his brother conversed at the door to the hut.

Still surprised at what he had seen, Martim did not move his eyes from the deep cave that the foot of the old pajé had opened in the floor of the hut. A muted sound, like the echo of waves breaking on the beach, rumbled there.

The Christian mused; he could not believe that the god of the Tabajaras had given his priest so much power.

Seeing what was taking place in the foreigner's soul, Araquém lit his pipe and grasped the *maracá*[6]: "It is time to appease the wrath of Tupã and still the voice of the thunder."

Saying this, he left the hut.

Then Iracema approached the youth; her lips bore a smile, her eyes rejoiced.

"The heart of Iracema is like *abati*,[7] rice in the water of the river. No one will harm the white warrior in the hut of Araquém."

"Withdraw from the enemy, maiden of the Tabajaras," answered the foreigner with severity in his voice.

Suddenly turning away, he avoided the maiden's gentle, pained eyes.

"What has Iracema done that the white warrior averts his eyes, as if she were a worm of the earth?"

The maiden's words echoed gently in Martim's heart. It is thus that the murmurs of the breeze echo in the palm fronds. The youth was displeased with himself, and felt compassion for her: "Do you not hear, beautiful maiden?" he exclaimed, pointing to the roaring cavern.

"It is the voice of Tupã!"

"Your god spoke through the mouth of the pajé: 'If the virgin of Tupã abandons to the white warrior the flower of her body, she will die!'"

Iracema bowed her head wearily: "It is not the voice of Tupã that your heart hears, warrior from far-off lands; it is the song of the yellow-haired maiden who calls you!"

The strange noise coming from the depths of the earth suddenly ceased; so great was the silence in the hut that the blood could be heard pulsing in the warrior's arteries, and the sigh trembling on the maiden's lips.

XII

The day darkened; it was now night. The pajé had returned to the hut; stepping again upon the thick stone slab, with it he closed the mouth of the cavern. Caubi had also arrived from the great village, where he had withdrawn with his brother warriors after they had scoured the forest in search of the Pitiguara enemy.

In the middle of the hut, between the hammocks strung in a square, Iracema spread the mat of carnauba and on it served what remained of the hunt and the store of wine from the last moon. Only the Tabajara warrior found any savor in the supper, for the wormwood that sorrow squeezes from the heart did not embitter his lips.

The pajé filled the pipe with the herb of Tupã; the foreigner breathed the pure air of night to cool his restive blood; the maiden was distilling her soul like the honey from a comb, in the persistent sobs that broke from her tremulous lips.

Caubi left for the great village; the pajé swallowed the breaths of smoke that makes ready the mystery of the sacred rite.

There rose in the still of night a vibrant cry that ascended to the heavens.

Martim lifted his head and tilted his ear. Another clamor like the first resounded. The warrior spoke softly, only for the maiden's ear: "Did you hear, Iracema, the song of the gull?"

"Iracema heard the cry of a bird she does not know."

"It is the *atiati*, the seagull, and you are a maiden of the mountains who has never descended to the white beaches where the waves break."

"The beaches belong to the Pitiguaras, lords of the palm trees."

The warriors of the great nation that inhabited the edge of the sea called themselves Pitiguaras, lords of the valley; but the Tabajaras, their enemies, mockingly nicknamed them Potiguaras, shrimp eaters.

Iracema feared offending the white warrior; therefore, speaking of the Pitiguaras, she did not deny them the name they had taken for themselves.

The foreigner prudently held back for an instant the word from his lips, while he reflected: "The seagull's song is the war cry of brave Poti, the friend of your guest!"

The maiden shuddered for her brothers. The fame of brave Poti, brother of Jacaúna, rose from the riverbanks to the peak of the Ibiapaba: rare was the hut where the cry of vengeance had not roared against him, for each blow of his stalwart club had laid a Tabajara warrior in his *camucim*.

Iracema thought that Poti was coming at the head of his warriors to free his friend. Beyond doubt, it was he who had made the conch from the beaches thunder again, at the moment of combat. It was in a tone that mingled gentleness and sorrow that she replied, "The foreigner is saved; the brothers of Iracema are going to die, because she will say nothing."

"Dismiss that sorrow from your soul. The foreigner, when he departs from your lands, Tabajara maiden, will not leave in them a trail of blood like the famished jaguar."

Iracema took the white warrior's hand and kissed it.

"Your smile, daughter of the pajé, has erased the memory of the evil they would do me."

Martim rose and walked to the door.

"Where does the white warrior go?"

"To meet Poti."

"Araquém's guest cannot leave this hut, because Irapuã's warriors will kill him."

"A warrior asks protection only of God and his weapons. He has no need for old men and women to defend him."

"What can one warrior alone avail against a thousand? Brave and strong is the anteater, which the wild cats bite and, because they are many, do him in. Your weapons reach only as far as the shadow of your body; their weapons fly as high and as straight as the sparrow hawk."

"Every warrior has his day."

"You do not want Iracema to die, yet you want her to let you die!"

Martim was confused.

"Iracema will go to the meeting with the Pitiguara chief and bring her guest the words of the friendly warrior."

The pajé finally emerged from his meditation. The gourd rattled in his right hand; the small bells tinkled to his slow, rigid step.

He called his daughter aside: "If Irapuã's warriors attack the hut, lift the stone and hide the foreigner in the bosom of the earth."

"The guest must not be alone; wait until Iracema returns. The *inhuma* has not yet sung."

The old man sat in the hammock again. The maiden left, closing the door to the hut.

XIII

Araquém's daughter proceeded through the darkness; she stopped and listened.

For the third time, the seagull's cry echoed in her ear; she went straight to the place from which it came. She reached the edge of a lake; her eyes searched the darkness, and she saw nothing of what she sought.

The gentle voice, soft as the hummingbird's drone, murmured, "Poti the Warrior, your white brother calls to you through Iracema's mouth."

Only the echo answered her.

"The daughter of your enemies comes to you, because the foreigner loves you, and she loves the foreigner."

The smooth surface of the lake parted, and a form appeared, which swam to the bank and emerged.

"It was Martim who sent you, for you know the name of Poti, his brother in warfare."

"Speak, Pitiguara chief; the white warrior awaits."

"Go to him and say that Poti has come to save him."

"He knows; and sent me to you."

"The words of Poti will leave his mouth only for his brother's ear."

"Wait then until Araquém departs and the hut is empty; I will guide you to the foreigner's presence."

"Never, daughter of the Tabajaras, has a Pitiguara warrior crossed the threshold of an enemy's hut, if not as a conqueror. Bring the warrior from the sea here."

"The vengeance of Irapuã sniffs around Araquém's hut. Has the foreigner's brother brought enough Pitiguara warriors to defend and save him?"

Poti reflected.

"Speak, maiden of the mountains, of what has happened in your lands after the warrior from the sea arrived there."

Iracema related how the wrath of Irapuã had become enraged against the foreigner, until the voice of Tupã, summoned by the pajé, had calmed his fury.

"The anger of Irapuã is like the bat: it flees from the light and flies in darkness."

Poti's hand suddenly hushed the maiden's lips; his words seemed like a sigh: "Hold your voice and your breath, maiden of the forest; the enemy's ear listens in the shadows."

The leaves rustled quietly, as if the mountain tinamou were moving there. A sound, coming from the edge of the wood, was running through the valley.

Brave Poti, gliding through the grass like the agile shrimp from which he had taken his name and his energy, disappeared into the deep lake. The water issued no murmur and closed its limpid waves over him.

Iracema returned to the hut; en route her eyes discerned the shadows of many warriors who crept along the ground like toads.

Seeing her enter, Araquém left.

The Tabajara maiden told Martim what she had heard from Poti; the Christian warrior sprang up to rush to the defense of his Pitiguara brother. Iracema encircled his neck with her lovely arms: "The chieftain has no need of you; he is the son of the waters, and the waters protect him. Later the foreigner will hear his friend's words."

"Iracema, it is time for your guest to leave the pajé's hut and the lands of the Tabajara. He does not fear Irapuã's warriors: he fears the eyes of Tupã's virgin."

"They will flee from you."

"Let the foreigner flee from them, as the nighthawk flees from the morning star."

Martim took a step.

"Go, ungrateful warrior; go and kill your brother first, then yourself. Iracema will follow you to the joyful lands to which go the shades of those who die."

"Kill my brother you say, cruel maiden."

"Your trail will lead the enemy to where the warrior of the valley hides."

The Christian stopped in the middle of the hut, where he stood, silent and motionless. Iracema, fearful of staring at him, looked at the warrior's shadow that the flames cast on the venerable walls of the hut.

The woolly dog, lying near the embers, gave signs of the approach of friendly people. The door, woven from carnauba stalks, was opened from outside. Caubi entered.

"The cashew wine disturbed the warriors' spirit; they come against the foreigner."

The maiden sprang up: "Lift the stone that seals Tupã's throat, so it may hide the foreigner."

The Tabajara warrior, raising the enormous slab, turned it over on the ground.

"Son of Araquém, lie down at the door of the hut and never again rise from the ground if a warrior steps over your body."

Caubi obeyed; the maiden closed the door.

A short time went by. The noise of warriors reverberated near at hand; the angry voices of Irapuã and Caubi engaged each other.

"They come; but Tupã will save his guest."

At that instant, as if the god of thunder had heard his virgin's words, the cavern, initially silent, resounded with a muffled roar.

"Listen! It is the voice of Tupã."

Iracema grasped the foreigner's hand and took him to the edge of the cavern. They disappeared into the bowels of the earth.

XIV

The Tabajara warriors, excited by their copious libations of foaming cashew wine, become enflamed at the words of Irapuã, who had so many times led them into combat, and to victory.

Wine slakes the body's thirst but provokes another, greater, thirst in the fierce soul. They roared vengeance against the bold foreigner who by defying their weapons offended the god of their fathers, and the chieftain of war, the first among Tabajara men.

They stamped their feet in fury and plunged into the shadows: the reddish light of the *ubiratā*,[1] the ironwood, glowing in the distance, led them to Araquém's hut. From time to time, those who first came to watch the enemy rose from the ground.

"The pajé is in the forest!" they whispered.

"And the foreigner?" asked Irapuã.

"In the hut with Iracema."

The chieftain leapt forward fearsomely and went

to the door of the hut, and with him his brave warriors.

Caubi's shadow filled the opening to the door; his weapons protected before him the space of a *maracajá's*[2] spring.

"Vile warriors are those who attack in a pack like the *caititus*.[3] The jaguar,[4] lord of the forest, and the *anajê*,[5] lord of the clouds, combat the enemy alone."

"May the unclean mouth that raises its voice against the bravest warrior of the Tabajara warriors bite the dust."

With these words, Irapuã's arm raised the implacable club, but stayed the blow: the bowels of the earth roared again, as they had roared when Araquém invoked the awesome voice of Tupã.

The warriors raised a fearful outcry, and, surrounding their chieftain, took him from the doleful place and from the wrath of Tupã that had been incited against them.

Caubi stretched out again in the threshold of the door; his eyes closed, but his subtle ear was alert in sleep.

The voice of Tupã had fallen silent.

Lost in the bowels of the earth, Iracema and the Christian descended the deep grotto. Suddenly, a voice echoing through the gallery filled his ears: "Does the warrior of the sea hear his brother's words?"

"It is Poti, your guest's friend," the Christian told the maiden.

Iracema shuddered: "He speaks through the mouth of Tupã."

Martim replied at last to the Pitiguara.

"The words of Poti enter his brother's soul."

"No other ear listens?"

"That of the maiden who has twice in one day defended your brother's life!"

"The woman is weak, the Tabajara a betrayer, and Jacaúna's brother is prudent."

Iracema sighed and rested her head on the youth's chest: "Master of Iracema, cover her ears so she does not hear."

Martim gently removed the graceful brow: "Let the Pitiguara chieftain speak; none but friendly and faithful ears will hear."

"You order, and Poti speaks. Before the sun rises on the mountains, the warrior of the sea must depart to the shores where the heron nests; the unmoving star will guide him. No Tabajara will follow him, for the Pitiguaras' war trumpet will roar from the direction of the mountains."

"How many Pitiguara warriors accompany their brave chief?"

"None; Poti came alone. When the evil spirits of the forest separated the warrior of the sea from his brother, Poti came following the trail. His heart did not let him return to call the warriors from their village, but he sent his faithful dog to great Jacaúna."

"The Pitiguara chief is alone: the war trumpet must not roar, for it will call against him all the Tabajara warriors."

"It must be so, to save his white brother. Poti will mock Irapuã, as he mocked when one hundred fought against you."

The pajé's daughter, who listened in silence, leaned her head against the Christian's ear: "Iracema desires to save you and your brother; she has a thought. The Pitiguara chieftain is brave and bold: Irapuã is cunning and treacherous like the *acauã*.[6] Before you arrive at the forest, you will fall, and your brother from the other side will fall with you."

"What can the Tabajara maiden do to save the foreigner and his brother?" asked Martim.

"The moon of flowers will soon come. It is the feast time, in which the Tabajara warriors spend the night in the sacred wood and from the pajé receive joyful dreams.

When all are asleep, the white warrior will depart from the lands of Ipu and from Iracema's eyes, but not from her soul."

Martim held the maiden to his chest, but quickly pushed her away. The touch of her body, as sweet as the white lily of the forest and as soft as the hummingbird's nest, pained his heart, for he remembered the terrible words of the pajé.

The Christian's voice conveyed to Poti the idea of Iracema; the Pitiguara chieftain, as prudent as the anteater, thought and then replied: "Wisdom has spoken through the Tabajara maiden's mouth. Poti will await the coming of the moon."

XV

The day was born and died. In Araquém's hut the
fire glowed, companion of the night. Slowly and
silently the stars, daughters of the moon, awaited their
absent mother's return as they moved in the blue of the
sky.

Martim rocked gently, and like the white hammock
that comes and goes, his desire oscillated from one
thought to another. There, the blond maiden awaited
him with her chaste affection; here, the dark maiden
smiled at him with her ardent love.

Iracema rested languidly against the rope of the
hammock; her dark, resplendent eyes, the tender eyes
of the thrush, sought out the foreigner and entered his
soul. The Christian smiled; the maiden quivered. Like
the *saí*[1] fascinated by the serpent, her sensual body in-
clined more and more, until it finally rested against the
warrior's chest.

The foreigner pressed her to his breast, and his avid

lips sought the lips that awaited him, to celebrate in that threshold to the soul the marriage of love.

In the darkened corner the old pajé, immersed in deep contemplation and distant from things of this world, groaned painfully. Had his heart felt a presentiment of what his eyes did not see? Or was it some dire presage for the race of his children that echoed in Araquém's soul?

No one knew.

The Christian pushed the Indian maiden from his breast. He would not leave a trail of misfortune in the hut where he had been made welcome. He closed his eyes so he would not see, and he filled his soul with the name and the veneration of his God: "Christ! . . . Christ!"

Serenity returned to the white warrior's breast, but each time his gaze rested on the Tabajara maiden, he felt a wave of impassioned flame running through his veins. It is thus that, when the unwise child stirs the coals of an intense fire, blazing sparks fly up to burn its cheeks.

The Christian closed his eyes, but in the shadow of his thoughts emerged the image of the maiden, perhaps more beautiful still. In vain he summoned sleep to his weary eyelids; they opened, despite his wishes.

From the heavens, an inspiration descended to his troubled thoughts: "Beautiful maiden of the forest, this is the last night that your guest will sleep in Araquém's hut, where it were better he had never been, for your good and his own. Let his sleep be joyful and happy."

"Order; Iracema will obey you. What can she do for your happiness?"

The Christian spoke softly, so the old pajé would not hear: "The virgin of Tupã keeps the dreams of the *jurema*, which are sweet and delicious!"

A sad smile afflicted Iracema's lips: "The foreigner is going to live forever at the white maiden's waist;[2] never again will his eyes see Araquém's daughter, and yet he

49

would have sleep close his eyes and have dreams take him to the land of his brothers!"

"Sleep is the warrior's rest," said Martim, "and dreams the soul's happiness. The foreigner does not wish to take with him the sorrow of the land that welcomed him, nor to leave it in the heart of Iracema!"

The maiden remained motionless.

"Go, and return with the wine of Tupã."

When Iracema returned, the pajé was no longer in the hut; the maiden took from her bosom the vessel that she carried hidden under the cotton *carioba*[3] interwoven with feathers. Martim seized it from her hands and gulped down the drops of the bitter green liquor.

Now he could be with Iracema and gather from her lips the kisses that luxuriated there among smiles, like fruit in the flower's corolla. He could love her and imbibe the honey and perfume from that love without leaving poison in the maiden's breast.

Pleasure was life, for he felt it more strongly, more intensely; evil was a dream and an illusion, for he possessed nothing save the image of the maiden.

Iracema had moved away, burdened and sighing.

The arms of the sleeping warrior opened, and his lips; the maiden's name was gently intoned.

The *juriti*, wandering through the forest, hears the tender cooing of its mate; it beats its wings and flies to find shelter in its warm nest. So did the maiden of the interior nestle in the warrior's arms.

When morning came, it still found Iracema enfolded there, like a butterfly that has slept in the bosom of the shapely cactus. On her lovely countenance, abashment had kindled a vivid scarlet, and like the first ray of sun glittering among the red clouds of morning, on her burning cheeks shone a wife's first smile, the dawn of a love come to fruition.

The *jandaia* had flown with the break of day, never to return to the hut.

Seeing the maiden united to his heart, Martim thought he was still dreaming; he closed his eyes and reopened them.

The warriors' battle cry, reverberating through the valley, plucked him from the sweet error: he sensed he was no longer dreaming, but living. His cruel hand stifled on the maiden's lips the kiss that fluttered there.

"Iracema's kisses are sweet in dreams; the white warrior has filled his soul with them. In life, the lips of Tupã's virgin are bitter and wound like the *jurema* thorn."

Araquém's daughter concealed the happiness in her heart. She became shy and restless, like the bird that foresees the tempest on the horizon. She moved quickly away and departed.

The waters of the river bathed the chaste body of the new bride.

Tupã no longer had his virgin in the land of the Tabajaras.

XVI

T he white disk of the moon rose on the horizon.
The brilliant sunlight paled the virgin of the sky,
as the love of the warrior fades the color from the
cheeks of his wife.

"Jaci![1] . . . Our mother!" exclaimed the Tabajara
warriors.

And, brandishing their bows, with a rain of arrows
they launched to the skies the song of the reborn
moon: "The mother of warriors has come to the heav-
ens; she turns her face to see her children. She brings
the waters that fill the rivers and the cashew fruit.

"The bride of the sun has come; she has smiled on
the virgins of the earth, her daughters. The gentle light
ignites love in the warriors' hearts and makes fertile
the young mother's breast."

Evening fell.

The women and the children rested in the vast
square; the young men, who had not yet won their

name in war for some brilliant feat, roamed in the valley.

The warriors followed Irapuã to the sacred wood where the pajé and his daughter awaited them with the mystery of the *jurema*. Iracema had already lit the fires of joy.[2] Araquém stood immobile and ecstatic in the center of a cloud of smoke.

Each warrior who arrived placed at his feet an offering to Tupã. One brought a succulent game animal; another, manioc flour; yet another, the tasty roasted *traíra* fish. The old pajé, for whom these gifts were brought, received them disdainfully.

When all were seated around the great fire, the minister of Tupã commanded silence with a gesture, and thrice shouting the terrible name, filled himself with the god, which inhabited him: "Tupã! . . . Tupã! . . . Tupã!"

From one deep valley to the next, the sound re-echoed into the distance.

Iracema arrived with the vessel filled with green liquor. Araquém determined each warrior's dream and distributed the wine of the *jurema*, which transported the brave Tabajaras to heaven.

One brave, a great hunter, dreamed that deer and cavies dash to meet his arrows and transfix themselves upon them; weary at last of inflicting injury, he digs in the earth a *bucã*,[3] the smoke pit, and roasts such a large amount of game that a thousand warriors would not finish it in a year.

Another, fiery in loves, dreamed that the most beautiful Tabajara maidens leave their fathers' huts and follow him, captives of his desire. Never did the hammock of any chieftain lull to sleep more voluptuous caresses than those he enjoys in that ecstasy.

The hero dreamed of tremendous struggles and horrible combat, from which he emerges the victor, filled with glory and fame. The old man was reborn in his numerous offspring, and like the dry trunk from which bursts forth a hardy new hedge, still covered himself in flowers.

All felt happiness so vivid and unbroken, that in the space of a single night they thought they had lived many moons. Mouths murmured: gestures spoke; and the pajé, who saw and heard everything, gathered the secret from the innermost recesses of the soul.

Iracema, after offering the chieftains the liquor of Tupã, departed from the wood. The ritual did not permit her to attend the warriors' sleep and hear the speaking of dreams.

She went from there straightaway to the hut, where Martim awaited her.

"Take your weapons, white warrior. It is time to depart."

"Lead me to where my brother Poti is."

The maiden traversed the valley; the Christian followed her. They came to the side of the cliff, which ended at the edge of the lake in a verdant thicket.

"Call your brother!"

Martim made the seagull's call. The stone that sealed the entrance to the cave fell, and the form of the warrior Poti appeared in the shadows.

The two brothers touched each other, brow to brow, chest to chest, to express that together they had but one mind and one heart.

"Poti is gladdened to see his brother, whom the evil spirit of the forest bore away from his sight."

"Happy is the warrior who has at his side a friend like brave Poti; all the warriors will envy him."

Iracema sighed, thinking that the affection of the Pitiguara was sufficient for the foreigner's happiness.

"The Tabajara warriors sleep. Araquém's daughter will guide the foreigners."

The maiden continued on her way, with the two warriors behind. When they had gone the distance that a heron covers in a flight, the Pitiguara chieftain became restive and whispered into the Christian's ear: "Order the pajé's daughter to return to her father's hut. She slows the warriors' progress."

Martim trembled, but the voice of caution and friendship penetrated his heart. He went to Iracema and summoned from within him his most tender tone to assuage the maiden's longing: "The deeper the plant's roots go into the earth, the more difficult to wrest it free. Each step that Iracema takes on the path of departure is a root she casts into the heart of her guest."

"Iracema would accompany you to where the lands of the Tabajara end, to return with peace in her heart."

Martim did not answer. They continued to walk, and with them traveled the night: the stars faded, and the coolness of dawn brought cheer to the forest. The raiment of the morn, as white as cotton, appeared in the heavens.

Poti looked at the woods and stopped. Martim understood and told Iracema: "Your guest no longer walks the land of the Tabajara. It is time that you leave him."

XVII

Iracema placed her hand on the white warrior's chest: "The daughter of the Tabajaras has left the land of her fathers; now she can speak."

"What secret do you keep inside your heart, beautiful maiden of the forest?"

"Iracema can no longer part from the foreigner."

"It is necessary, daughter of Araquém. Return to the hut of your aged father, who waits for you."

"Araquém has a daughter no more."

Martim replied with a harsh, severe motion: "No warrior of my race has ever left the hut of his host bereft of its happiness. Araquém will embrace his daughter, lest he curse the ungrateful foreigner."

The maiden lowered her head; covering herself with the long, dark braids that fell over her bosom, folding her lovely arms over her body, she withdrew into her propriety. Thus does the rosy cactus, blossomed into beautiful flower, envelop in a bud its perfumed heart.

"Iracema will accompany you, white warrior, for she is now your wife."

Martim trembled.

'The evil spirits of the night have clouded Iracema's soul."

"The white warrior was dreaming when Tupã abandoned his virgin. The pajé's daughter betrayed the secret of the *jurema*."

The Christian hid his face from the light.

"God! . . ." exclaimed his tremulous lips.

Both remained silent and motionless.

Finally, Poti said, "The Tabajara warriors awaken."

The maiden's heart, like the foreigner's, was deaf to the voice of prudence. The sun rose on the horizon, and its majestic eye descended from the hills to the forest. Poti stood, silent and motionless as a severed tree trunk, waiting until his brother would depart.

It was Iracema who first spoke: "Come: until you tread the shores of the Pitiguara your life is in danger."

Silently, Martim followed the maiden, who moved swiftly among the trees like the wild agouti. Sorrow oppressed his heart, but the wave of perfumes that the beautiful Tabajara's passing left on the breeze incited love in the warrior's breast. His pace was slow, and his chest heaved.

Poti pondered. In his young man's head lived the spirit of an *abaeté*,[1] a good and wise man. The Pitiguara chieftain was thinking that love is like cashew wine, which if drunk in moderation strengthens the warrior and taken in excess fells the heroic heart. He knew how swift were the Tabajaras' feet, and he awaited the moment of dying in the defense of his friend.

When the shadows of afternoon were saddening the day, the Christian halted in the middle of the woods. Poti lit the fire of hospitality. The maiden unfolded the white cotton hammock with fringe of toucan feathers and hung it from the boughs of the tree: "Husband of Iracema, your hammock awaits you."

Araquém's daughter went to sit at a distance, on the root of a tree, like the solitary doe driven from its retreat by its thankless mate. The Pitiguara warrior disappeared into the dense foliage.

Martim became silent and melancholy, like the tree trunk from which the wind has torn the lovely vine that entwined it. The passing breeze bore a murmur: "Iracema!"

It was the mate's cry; the doe, angry, entered the welcoming retreat.

The forest distilled a soft fragrance and breathed harmonious arpeggios: the sighs of the heart radiated into the murmurs of the wild. It was the festival of love and the wedding song.

The light of morning filtered through the dense woodland. The grave, sonorous voice of Poti resounded in the humming of the woods: "The Tabajara walk in the forest!"

Iracema tore herself from the arms that enfolded her and from the lips that held her captive; springing from the hammock like the fleet tinamou, she seized her husband's weapons and with them traversed the forest.

From time to time, wise Poti listened to the bowels of the earth; his head moved heavily from side to side like the cloud that, in the divers gusts of the coming tempest, sways atop the cliff.

"What does the ear of the warrior Poti hear?"

"It hears the fleet step of the Tabajara. He comes like the peccary breaking through the forest."

"The Pitiguara warrior is the ostrich that flies above the earth; we will follow him like his wings," said Iracema.

The chieftain again shook his head: "While the warrior of the sea was sleeping, the enemy ran. Those first to leave already advance far with the ends of their bow."

Shame gnawed at Martim's heart: "Let the chieftain Poti flee and save Iracema. Only the bad warrior should die, he who heeded not his brother's voice and his wife's entreaty."

Martim abjured: "It was not the soul of the warrior of the sea that spoke. Poti and his brother have a single life."

Iracema's lips did not speak: they smiled.

XVIII

The woodland trembled to the noise of the Tabajaras' run.

Great Irapuã, at their head, appeared among the trees. His reddish gaze spied the white warrior between clouds of blood: the angry roar of the jaguar erupted from his cavernous chest.

The Tabajara chieftain and his men were about to hurl themselves upon the fugitives like the angry wave that breaks on the Knoll of Sand.

It was then that the wild dog barked.

Martim's friend shouted with joy: "Poti's dog guides the warriors from his village to his rescue."

The hoarse conch shell resounded through the forest. Great Jacaúna,[1] lord of the seashore, was arriving from the river of herons with his finest warriors.

The Pitiguaras received the initial thrust of the enemy on the sharp points of their arrows, which they launched from their bows in sheaves, as the *cuandu*[2] the quills from its body. Immediately, the war cry sounded, the distance narrowed, and the battle was waged face to face.

Jacaúna attacked Irapuã. The horrific combat ensued, enough for ten braves, without exhausting the strength of the great chieftains. When the two clubs met, the entire battle shuddered as a single warrior, to the very entrails.

Iracema's brother came directly at the foreigner who had torn the daughter of Araquém from the welcoming hut; the scent of vengeance guided him: the sight of his sister aroused rage in his breast. The warrior Caubi fell upon the enemy with fury.

Iracema, at the side of her warrior and husband, saw Caubi from a distance and spoke thus: "Master of Iracema, hear the plea of your slave; do not shed the blood of the son of Araquém. If the warrior Caubi must die, let him die by this hand, not by yours."

Martim turned terrified eyes on the maiden: "Iracema would kill her brother?"

"Iracema would sooner have Caubi's blood stain her hand than yours; for Iracema's eyes look upon you, and not upon herself."

The battle waged among the warriors. Caubi fought furiously; the Christian only defended himself, but the arrow ready in his wife's bow protected the warrior's life against the enemy's thrusts.

Poti had already felled old Andira and all the warriors who met in battle his brave club. Martim left the son of Araquém and advanced upon Irapuã: "Jacaúna is a great chieftain; his war necklace[3] thrice encircles his chest. The Tabajara belongs to the white warrior."

"Vengeance is the warrior's honor, and Jacaúna holds dear the friend of Poti."

The great Pitiguara chieftain withdrew his formidable club. Irapuã and Martim engaged in combat. The Christian's sword, striking the savage's club, shattered.

The Tabajara chieftain advanced against the enemy's defenseless chest.

Iracema hissed like the rattlesnake and flung herself against the fury of the Tabajara warrior. The implacable weapon hesitated in the powerful right hand of the chieftain and his arm dropped, lifeless.

The joyous cry of victory sounded. The Pitiguara warriors led by Jacaúna and Poti swept through the forest. Fleeing, the Tabajaras conducted their chieftain from the hatred of the daughter of Araquém, which could fell him, as the *jandaia* fells the tall coconut palm by pecking at its core.

Iracema's eyes, perusing the forest, saw the ground strewn with the bodies of her brothers, and in the distance the party of Tabajara warriors fleeing in a dark cloud of dust. The blood that stained red the earth was the same proud blood that burned her cheeks with shame.

Tears bedewed her lovely countenance.

Martim walked away lest he dishonor Iracema's sorrow.

XIX

P oti returned from his pursuit of the enemy. His
eyes were filled with happiness at seeing the white
warrior safe.

The faithful dog followed closely behind him, still
licking from the hair of its snout the Tabajara blood on
which it had satiated itself; its master caressed it,
pleased at its courage and dedication. It had been he
who had saved Martim by so diligently bringing Ja-
caúna's warriors there.

"The evil spirits of the forest may once again sepa-
rate the white warrior from his Pitiguara brother. The
dog will go with you from this time forward, so that
even from far away Poti can come at your call."

"But the dog is your faithful companion and friend."

"A greater friend will he be to Poti by serving his
brother rather than him. You will call him Japi,[1] and he
will be the swift foot by which from far away we each
run to the other."

Jacaúna gave the sign to depart.

The Pitiguara warriors set out for the happy margins of the river where the herons drink; there stood the great village of the lords of the plains.

The sun set and rose again in the sky. The warriors arrived to the place where the mountain range sloped to the inland: they had passed the part of the mountain that, because it was devoid of trees and sheared like the cavy, the people of Tupã called Ibiapina.²

Poti took the Christian to where a leafy *jatobá*³ grew, which faced the trees of the highest pinnacle of the sierra and which when lashed by a gust of wind seemed to brush the sky with its immense crown.

"At this place was your brother born," said the Pitiguara.

Martim embraced the fraternal tree: "*Jatobá* that saw my brother's birth, the foreigner embraces thee."

"May lightning fell thee, tree of the warrior Poti, when his brother abandons him."

Then the chieftain spoke these words: "When Jacaúna was not yet a warrior, Jatobá, the greatest of chiefs, led the Pitiguaras to victory. As soon as the great waters ran, he traveled to the sierra. Arriving there, he ordered the village built, to be close to the enemy and more often defeat him. The same moon that saw him arrive lit the hammock where Saí, his wife, gave him another warrior of his blood. The moonlight passed through the leaves of the *jatobá*, and the smile on the lips of the stalwart man who had taken its name and strength."

Iracema approached.

The turtledove, which pecks for food in the sand, if its mate retires, flutters from branch to branch, and coos so that its absent friend can reply. So too did the daughter of the forests roam about the hillsides, intoning her simple melodious song.

Martim received her with his soul glowing in his eyes, and, taking his wife at the side of his heart and his friend at the side of his strength, he returned to the huts of the Pitiguaras.

XX

The moon waxed. For three suns Martim and Iracema had been in the lands of the Pitiguaras, lords of the banks of the Camucim and Acaracu. The foreigners had their hammock in Jacaúna's vast hut. The brave chieftain reserved for himself the pleasure of hosting the white warrior.

Poti left his village so that, in the hut of his brother in blood, he might accompany his brother in war and enjoy the instants that remained for the friendship in the heart of the warrior of the sea.

Shadow had fled the face of the earth, and Martim saw that it had not yet withdrawn from the face of his wife since the day of combat.

"Sorrow dwells in Iracema's soul!"

"Happiness for your wife comes from you alone; when your eyes turn away from her, her own are filled with tears."

"Why does the daughter of the Tabajaras weep?"

"This is the village of the Pitiguaras, enemies of my people. Iracema's eyes have seen the skulls of her brothers on the stockade spikes; her ears have heard the death song of the Tabajara captives; her hands have touched the weapons stained with the blood of her fathers."

His wife placed both hands on the warrior's shoulders and leaned against his chest: "Iracema bears all for her warrior and master. The sugar apple is sweet and tasty, but when it is bruised it sours. Your wife wants her love to fill your heart with the sweetness of honey."

"Let peace return to the soul of the daughter of the Tabajara; she will leave the village of her people's enemies."

The Christian went to Jacaúna's hut. The great chieftain was heartened to see his guest; but the joy quickly fled from his warrior's face. Martim said, "The white warrior is leaving your hut, great chief."

"Is there something you lack in Jacaúna's village?"

"Nothing is lacking to your guest. He was happy here; but the voice of the heart summons him to other places."

"Depart, then, and take whatever you need for the journey. May Tupã give you strength and bring you again to the hut of Jacaúna so he may celebrate your welcome."

Poti arrived. Learning that the warrior of the sea would depart, he said, "Your brother goes with you."

"Poti's warriors have need of their chief."

"If you do not want them to go with Poti, Jacaúna will lead them to victory."

"Poti's hut will become empty and sad."

"Empty and sad is the heart of your brother away from you."

The warrior of the sea left the banks of the river of herons and traveled toward the lands where the sun sets. His wife and his friend accompanied his trek.

He passed beyond the fertile mountain where the abundance of fruit spawned flies in great number, from which came its name, Meruoca.[1]

They traversed the fields bathed by the river of herons and saw on the distant horizon a tall mountain range. Day came to its end; a dark cloud flew from the direction of the sea: it was the vultures that had fed on carrion on the beaches and at night returned to their nest.

The travelers slept there, in Uruburetama.[2] With the second sun they arrived at the banks of the river, which arises at the slopes of the sierra and descends the plain, coiling like a snake. Its continuous turns deceived the pilgrim at every step as he followed its tortuous course; for this reason it was called the Mundaú.[3]

Moving along the cool banks, Martim saw the next day the green seas and white shores, where the murmuring waves sometimes sob and at other times rage with fury, breaking into foamy flakes.

The white warrior's eyes opened wide at the vast immensity: he sighed. That sea also kissed the white sands of Potengi,[4] his birthplace, where he had first seen the light of the Americas.

He plunged into the waves and thought of bathing his body in the waters of his homeland as he had bathed his soul in his longing for it.

Iracema felt her heart weeping, but the warrior's smile soon appeased it.

Meanwhile, from atop a boulder, Poti speared the tasty shrimp that sported in the small bay of Mundaú, and prepared the roasting sticks for the meal.

XXI

The sun was already descending from the heights of the sky.

The travelers arrived at the mouth of the river, where the savory *traíra*[1] grow in great abundance: its beaches are populated by the tribe of fishermen, of the great Pitiguara nation.

They received the foreigners with generous hospitality, which was a law of their religion, and Poti with the respect due such a celebrated warrior, brother to Jacaúna, the greatest chieftain of the mighty Pitiguara people.

To rest the travelers, and to accompany them in the leave-taking, the chief of the tribe received Poti, Martim, and Iracema on his raft and, unfurling the sail to the wind, carried them far along the coast.

The fishermen on their rafts followed the chief and stirred the air with the song of longing and with the murmurs of the shell-flute, which imitates the sobbing of the wind.

Beyond the sandbar of the Piroquara,[2] nearer the sierra, was the tribe of hunters. They occupied the banks of the Soipé,[3] covered with woodland where the deer, the plump cavies, and the tender guan abounded. Thus the inhabitants of these banks named them "land of the hunt."

The chieftain of the hunters, Jaguaraçu, had his hut at the edge of the lake that the river forms near the sea. There, the travelers found the same welcome they had received from the fishermen.

After they left the Soipé, the travelers crossed the Taíba river, on whose banks wandered packs of wild pigs; further on flowed the Cauípe,[4] where excellent cashew wine was produced.

The next day, they saw a beautiful river that emerged from the sea, etching a basin in the living rock.

Beyond, on the horizon loomed a high elevation of sand with the whiteness of sea foam. The towering cape looked like the bald head of the condor, awaiting there the tempest that comes from the farthest reaches of the ocean.

"Does Poti know the great hill of sand?" the Christian asked.

"Poti knows all the land that belongs to the Pitiguaras, from the banks of the great river that forms an arm of the sea[5] to the riverbank where the jaguar dwells. He has been to the top of the Mocoripe,[6] and from there seen the movement of the large boats of the white warriors, your enemies, who are on the Mearim."

"Why do you call the great hill of sand Mocoripe?"

"The fisherman of the beach, who goes out on the raft, there where the brown-headed gull flies, feels sadness far from land and from the hut where sleep the children of his blood. When he returns and his eyes first spy the hill of sand, pleasure comes back to his heart. That is why he says that the hill of sand brings joy."

"The fisherman speaks wisely; for like him your brother was gladdened to see the mount of sand."

Martim ascended with Poti to the top of the Mocoripe. Iracema, accompanying her husband with her eyes, wandered like the *jaçana* bird about the lovely bay that there the earth made to receive the sea.

On her way, she gathered the sweet cashew fruit that slakes the warriors' thirst, and picked up pretty shells to adorn her neck.

The travelers spent three days on the Mocoripe. Then Martim turned his steps onward. His wife and his friend returned to the mouth of the river, whose banks were flooded and covered with mangroves. The sea, penetrating it, formed a bay filled with crystalline water and carved out of the stone like a sarcophagus.

As he explored this place, the Christian warrior began to ponder. Till then, he had traveled without a destination, his movements unplanned; his only intention was to leave behind the villages of the Tabajaras and thus wrest the sorrow from Iracema's heart. The Christian knew from experience that a journey appeases longing, for the soul sleeps when the body walks. Now, sitting on the beach, he reflected.

Poti appeared: "The white warrior thinks; his brother's heart is open to receive his thought."

"Your brother is thinking that this place is better than the banks of the Jaguaribe for the village of the warriors of your race. In these waters the large boats that come from far-off lands could hide from the wind and the sea: from here they would go to the Mearim to destroy the white *tapuias*,[7] allies of the Tabajaras, enemies of your nation."

The Pitiguara chieftain meditated and replied: "Go and find your warriors. Poti will build his village next to the *mairi*[8] of his brother."

Iracema approached. The Christian gestured to the Pitiguara chieftain for silence.

"Her husband's voice falls quiet and his gaze is lowered when Iracema arrives. Would you have her withdraw?"

"Your husband would have you draw nearer, so that his voice and his eyes may penetrate more deeply into your soul."

The beautiful savage burst into smiles, as the flower yields to the budding fruit, and leaned against the warrior's shoulder.

"Iracema hears you."

"These lands are happy, and even more when Iracema dwells in them. What does your heart say?"

"His wife's heart is ever joyful beside her warrior and master."

Following the banks of the river, the Christian chose a place to build the hut. Poti cut stays from the trunks of carnauba trees; Araquém's daughter joined the palm fans to cover the roof and walls; Martim dug the earth and made the door from strips of bamboo.

When night came, the husband and wife strung the hammock in their new hut, and their friend slept on the porch that faced the rising sun.

XXII

Poti greeted his friend and spoke these words: "Be-
fore the father of Jacaúna and Poti, the brave war-
rior Jatobá, ruled all the Pitiguara warriors, the great
war club of the nation was in the right hand of Ba-
tuireté,[1] the supreme chief, father of Jatobá. He it was
who came along the beaches of the sea to the river of
the jaguar and expelled the Tabajara to the interior,
setting the limits of their land for each tribe; then he
penetrated the inland as far as the sierra that took his
name.

"When his stars were many,[2] so many that in his *ca-
mucim* there was no more room for the cashew nuts
that marked the number, his body bent toward the
ground, and his arm stiffened like the branch of the
unyielding ironwood; the light in his eyes dimmed.

"Then he summoned the warrior Jatobá[3] and said,
'My son, take the club of the Pitiguara nation. Tupã
does not want Batuireté to carry it into battle, for he

has taken away the strength from his body, the quickness from his arm, and the light from his eyes. But Tupã has been good to him, for he gave him a son like the warrior Jatobá.'

"Jatobá took the war club of the Pitiguaras. Batuireté picked up the staff of his old age and began to walk. He crossed the vast backlands until he came to the luxuriant plains where the waters flow that come from the regions of the night. When the old warrior dragged his body along the riverbanks, and the shadow over his eyes no longer allowed him to see the fruit on the trees or the birds in the air, he would say in sorrow, 'Oh! My times that were!'

"The people who heard him lamented the ruin of the great chieftain; and ever since, passing through those places, they would repeat his words, from which the river and the plains came to be called Quixeramobim.[4]

"Batuireté came along the path of the herons[5] to that sierra that you see in the distance, where he first dwelled. There on the pinnacle, the old warrior made his nest, as high as the hawk's, to live out the rest of his days in conversation with Tupã. His son already sleeps beneath the earth, and during the last moon he was meditating at the door of his hut, awaiting the night that brings the great sleep. All the Pitiguara chiefs, when they awaken to the call of war, go to ask the old man to teach them to vanquish, for no other warrior has ever known how to fight as did he. So the tribes now call him not by his name but the great sage of war, Maranguab.[6]

"The chieftain Poti goes to the sierra to see his mighty grandfather, but before the day dies he will be back in his brother's hut. Have you another desire?"

"The white warrior will accompany you to embrace the great chief of the Pitiguara, grandfather of his brother, and to tell the ancient one that he has been reborn in the son of his son."

Martim summoned Iracema, and they set out, guided by the Pitiguara, for the Maranguab range that rose on the horizon. They followed the course of the river until the place where it was joined by the Pirapora[7] stream.

The old warrior's hut was next to the beautiful waterfall, where the fish leap amid the bubbling foam. The waters there are cool and calm, like the sea breeze that in the still hours wafts between the coconut palms.

Batuireté was seated under one of the small caves over the waterfall, and the blazing sun fell on his head, devoid of hair and as wrinkled as the genipap fruit. Thus sleeps the *jabiru* stork on the edge of the lake.

"Poti has come to the hut of the great Maranguab, father of Jatobá, and has brought his white brother to see the grandest warrior of the nations."

The old man half opened his heavy eyelids and ran his lusterless gaze from his grandson to the foreigner. Then his chest heaved and his lips whispered: "Tupã has willed that before losing their sight these eyes should see the white hawk[8] beside the *narceja*."

The wise old man's head dropped to his chest, and he spoke nor moved no more.

Poti and Martim thought he was sleeping and respectfully moved away lest they disturb the repose of one who had done so much in his long lifetime. Iracema, who was bathing in the nearby waterfall, came to them bearing the purest of honeycombs on a taro leaf.

The foreigners wandered about the flowery slopes until the shadows of the mountain extended along the valley. Then they returned to the place where they had left Maranguab.

The old man was still in the same position, his head fallen onto his chest and his knees against his brow. Ants were crawling up his body, and small parrots were fluttering around him and settling on his bald scalp.

Poti placed his hand on the elder's skull and saw that he was no more; the warrior had died of old age. Then the Pitiguara chieftain intoned the death chant, and went into the hut to find the *camucim* that was overflowing with cashew nuts. Martim counted five times five handfuls.

Meanwhile, Iracema gathered in the forest the carapa with which to anoint the body of the old man, which his grandson's devoted hand enclosed in the *camucim*. The funeral vessel was hung from the roof of the hut.

After placing nettles at the door, to defend the abandoned hut against animals, Poti bade a sorrowful farewell to that place and with his companions returned to the edge of the sea.

The sierra where the hut had once been took the name of Maranguape, called thus because there reposed the sage of war.

XXIII

F our moons had lit the sky since Iracema had left the plains of Ipu, and for three she had dwelled on the beaches of the sea in the hut of her husband.

Joy resided in her soul. The daughter of the interior was happy, like the swallow that leaves its parents' nest and travels afar to build a new nest in the land where the season of flowers is beginning. Iracema too had found there on the ocean beaches a nest of love, her heart's new homeland.

Like the hummingbird flitting among the acacia flowers, she wandered about the pleasant meadows. The morning light would find her clinging to her husband's shoulder and smiling, like the vine that entwines the sturdy tree trunk and each morning bedecks it anew with a garland.

Martim left for the hunt with Poti. The maiden would separate herself from him at such times, the more ardently to desire the sight of him.

Nearby was a beautiful lake in the midst of the green meadow. The savage directed her agile steps there. It was the time of the morning bath; she dived into the water and swam with the white herons and the red *jaçanas*.

The Pitiguara warriors who came that way called the lake Porangaba, or lake of beauty, for in it bathed Iracema, the most beautiful daughter of Tupã's race.

And ever since that time mothers would come from far away to plunge their daughters in the waters of the Porangaba,[1] which had the virtue of imparting beauty to the maidens and making them to be loved by warriors.

After her bath, Iracema wandered about the sides of the Maranguab sierra, where the Jereraú,[2] the brook of the wild ducks, arose. There, in the cool shade grew the most delicious fruits in all the country; from them the maiden took a copious supply and waited, rocking under the boughs of the granadilla tree for Martim to return from the hunt.

At other times, it was not the Jereraú[2] that attracted her but, from the opposite side, the Sapiranga,[3] whose waters stung the eyes, as the pajés said. Close by was a copse of wine palms that formed in the midst of the plain a large island of beautiful palm trees.

Iracema was fond of the Muritiapuá,[4] where the wind sighed softly; there she would remove the husk from the red coconut to make a cooling drink sweetened with honey, and with it fill the vessel that would slake the warriors' thirst during the stillest part of the day.

One morning Poti led Martim to the hunt. They walked toward a sierra that rose beside the other, the Maranguab, its sister. The high summit is curved like the parrot's beak, and because of this the warriors called it Aratanha.[5] They climbed the slope of the Guaiúba[6] through which the waters descend to the valley, and arrived at the stream inhabited by cavies.

The sun was visible only at the parrot's beak when the hunters descended from Pacatuba[7] to the plain. In the distance they saw Iracema, who had come to await them at the shore of the Porangaba lake. She walked toward them with the proud step of the heron that stroll, at water's edge: over her *carioba* she wore a girdle of cassava flowers, a symbol of fecundity. A necklace of the same flowers encircled her neck and adorned her firm, quivering breasts.

She took her husband's hand and placed it against her lap: "Your blood already lives in Iracema's bosom. She will be the mother of your child."

"Child, you say?" exclaimed the Christian joyously.

He kneeled and, encircling her with his arms, kissed his wife's fertile bosom.

When he rose, Poti spoke: "The happiness of the youth is his wife and his friend; the first brings joy, the second gives strength. The warrior without a wife is like a tree without leaves or flowers: never will it see fruit. The warrior without a friend is like the solitary tree that the wind lashes in the middle of the plain: its fruit never ripens. The happiness of the man is his offspring, which are born of him and are his pride; each warrior that springs from his veins is one more bough that raises his name to the clouds, like the topmost part of the cedar. Beloved of Tupã is the warrior who has a wife, a friend, and many children; he has nothing more to desire but a death with glory."

Martim touched his chest to Poti's chest: "The heart of husband and friend have spoken through your mouth. The white warrior is happy, chieftain of the Pitiguaras, lords of the sea beaches; happiness was born for him in the land of palms, where vanilla perfumes the air; and it was generated in the blood of your race, whose face bears the color of the sun. The white warrior desires no other homeland but that of his son and of his heart."

At the break of dawn, Poti departed to gather *cara-juru* seeds, which yield a beautiful red dye, and the bark of the angico, from which is extracted the most lustrous black. On the way, his sure-sighted arrow brought down a wild duck that soared in the air. The warrior plucked the long feathers from its wings and, climbing the Mocoripe, sounded the war trumpet. The wind gusting from the sea carried into the distance, far into the distance, the hoarse sound. The shell-trumpet of the fishermen on the Trairi, and the horn of the hunters along the Soipé, answered.

Martim bathed in the river's waters and strolled along the beach to dry his body in the wind and sun. Beside him went Iracema, picking up the yellow ambergris[8] cast up by the sea. Each night his wife would perfume her body and the white hammock so that the warrior's love might take delight in it.

Poti returned.

XXIV

It was the custom of the race, the children of Tupã, for the warrior to wear on his body the color of his nation.

They would first draw black lines on the body, like those on the coat of the coati, from which came the name of that art of war-painting. They would also vary the colors, and many warriors customarily wrote the symbols of their deeds.

The foreigner, having adopted the homeland of his wife and his friend, must pass through that ceremony in order to become a red warrior, son of Tupã. With that intent, Poti had gone to find the necessary objects.

Iracema prepared the dyes. The chieftain, dipping the vanes of the feather, traced along the body the red and black lines that adorn the great Pitiguara nation. He then painted an arrow on the forehead and said, "Just as the arrow penetrates the hard trunk, so too the warrior's gaze penetrates the soul of the peoples."

On the arm he painted a hawk: "Just as the sparrow hawk falls from the heavens, so too falls the warrior's arm upon the enemy."

On the left foot he painted the root of the coconut palm: "Just as the small root secures to the earth the tall coconut palm, so too does the warrior's firm foot sustain his powerful body."

On the right foot he painted a wing: "Just as the swallow's wing parts the air, so too the warrior's fleet foot has no equal in the race."

Iracema took the vane of the feather and painted a bee on a tree leaf, her voice echoing between smiles: "Just as the bee makes its honey in the dark heart of the jacaranda, so too is sweetness in the bravest warrior's breast."

Martim opened his arms and his lips to receive the body and the soul of his wife.

"My brother is a great warrior of the Pitiguara nation: he needs a name in the language of his nation."

"Your brother's name is on his body, where your hand placed it."

"Coatiabo!"[1] exclaimed Iracema.

"You have spoken it: I am the painted warrior, the warrior of his wife and of his friend."

Poti gave to his friend the bow and club that are the warrior's noble arms. Iracema had woven for him the cockade and the feathered belt, the adornments of illustrious chieftains.

Araquém's daughter went to the hut to bring back the delicacies of the feast and the wines made from genipap and manioc. The warriors drank copiously and danced joyful dances. While they whirled around the fires of gladness, songs resounded.

Poti sang: "Like the snake that has two heads on a single body, so is the friendship of Coatiabo and Poti."

Iracema added: "Like the oyster that leaves not the rock even after death, so is Iracema at her husband's side."

The warriors said: "Like the *jatobá* in the forest, so is the warrior Coatiabo among his brother and his wife: its boughs embrace the boughs of the ironwood, and its shade protects the humble grass."

The fires of joy burned until morning came, and the warriors' feast continued as long.

XXV

For all the time that the ears of corn took to yellow, happiness dwelled in the hut.

One morning at daybreak, the Christian went to the edge of the sea. His soul was weary.

The hummingbird[1] drinks its fill of nectar and perfume, then sleeps in its white nest of down until the season of flowers returns the next year. Like the hummingbird, so too does the soul of the warrior saturate itself with happiness and have need of sleep and repose.

The hunt and the sallies about the mountains in the company of his friend, the caresses of his tender wife who awaited his return, and the pleasant *carbeto*,[2] or colloquy, on the porch of the hut no longer stirred in him the emotions of earlier times. His heart was restless.

While Iracema frolicked along the beach, the warrior's eyes turned from her to gaze upon the immensity of the sea.

They saw white wings that fluttered through the blue fields. The Christian knew it was a large boat with many sails, such as his brothers built; and longing for his homeland gripped his heart.

The sun rose high in the sky, and the warrior on the beach followed the fleeing sails with his gaze. In vain did his wife call him to the hut, in vain did she proffer to his eyes her graces and the finest fruits from the fields. The warrior did not move, until the sail had disappeared on the horizon.

Poti returned from the sierra, where for the first time he had gone alone. He had left serenity on his brother's countenance, and now found sorrow there. Martim went to greet him: "The great boat of the white foe passed on the sea. Your brother's eyes saw them winging to the banks of the Mearim, those allies of the Tupinambá, enemies of your race and mine."

"Poti is lord of a thousand bows; if such is your desire, he will go with you and his warriors to the banks of the Mearim to vanquish the white barbarians and their friends, the treacherous Tupinambá."

"When it is time, your brother will tell you."

The warriors entered the hut, where Iracema was. The sweet song had been stilled that day on his wife's lips. She sighed as she wove the fringe on the hammock of motherhood, wider and heavier than the matrimonial hammock.

Poti, seeing her thus occupied, said, "When the thrush sings, it is the time for love; when it falls silent, it makes the nest for its young: it is the time for work."

"My brother speaks like the frog when it announces the rain; but the thrush that makes its nest does not know if it will sleep in it."

Iracema's voice was a moan. Her gaze sought her husband. Martim was pondering: Iracema's words passed by him like the wind along the smooth face of the cliff, with neither echo nor sound.

The sun yet shone on the ocean shore, and the sands reflected the burning rays; but neither the light from heaven nor the light reflected from the earth could put to flight the shadow in the Christian's soul. The darkness in his visage grew ever greater.

A Pitiguara warrior, sent by Jacaúna to his brother Poti, arrived from the banks of the river of herons. He came following the trail of the travelers as far as the Trairi, where the fishermen had guided him to the hut.

Poti was alone on the porch; he rose and inclined his head to listen respectfully and gravely to the words sent by his brother through the mouth of the messenger: "The white barbarians who were on the Mearim have come through the woods to the beginning of the Ibiapaba, where they made an alliance with Irapuã to fight the Pitiguara nation. They will descend from the sierra to the banks of the river where the herons drink, and where you built the village of your warriors. Jacaúna calls you to defend the lands of our fathers: your people need their greatest warrior."

"Return to the banks of the Acaracu, and let not your foot rest until it treads the floor of Jacaúna's hut. When you arrive there, tell the great chief, 'Your brother is come to the village of his warriors.' And it will not be a lie."

The messenger departed.

Poti donned his weapons and set off for the plains, guided by Coatiabo's steps. He found him far away, wandering in the canebrake that borders the banks of Aquiraz.

"The white barbarians are on the Ibiapaba to help the Tabajaras to fight against Jacaúna. Your brother rushes to defend the land of his children, and the village where sleeps the *camucim* of his father. He will be able to conquer quickly, to return to your presence."

"Your brother goes with you. Nothing separates two warrior friends when the war trumpet sounds."

"You are great like the sea and kind like the sky."

They embraced, then departed facing into the direction of the rising sun.

XXVI

Trekking, ever trekking, the warriors reached the edge of a lake that stood in the plains.

The Christian suddenly stopped and turned his eyes in the direction of the sea: sorrow left his heart and rose to his face.

"My brother," said the chief, "your feet have put down roots in the land of love; stay here: Poti will soon return."

"Your brother will accompany you; so has he said, and his word is like the arrow of his bow: when it sounds, it arrives at its mark."

"Would you have Iracema go with you to the banks of the Acaracu?"

"We go to battle her brothers. The village of the Pitiguaras will hold for her only sorrow and pain. The daughter of the Tabajaras must stay."

"What then do you await?"

"Your brother is troubled because the daughter of the Tabajaras may become sorrowful and abandon the hut, without awaiting his return. Before departing, he desires to soothe his wife's spirit."

Poti reflected: "A woman's tears soften the warrior's heart as the dew of morning softens the earth."

"My brother is a great sage. Her husband should depart without seeing Iracema."

The Christian moved forward, but Poti told him to wait: from the quiver of arrows that Iracema had fletched with red and black feathers and hung on her husband's shoulder, he withdrew one.

The Pitiguara chieftain tensed his bow; the speeding arrow transpierced a large crab running along the edge of the lake, stopping only when the feathers allowed it to penetrate no farther.

The warrior planted the arrow in the ground with its impaled prey and turned to Coatiabo: "Now you can depart. Iracema will follow your trail; when she arrives here she will see your arrow and obey your will."

Martim smiled, and, breaking a twig of the passion-flower, the flower of remembrance, he entwined it about the shaft of the arrow and set off at last, followed by Poti.

The two warriors soon disappeared among the trees. The sun's heat had already dried their footprints at the shore of the lake. Restive, Iracema followed her husband's trail through the meadow as far as the plains. Soft shadows were covering the fields when she came to the lakeside.

Her eyes, spying her husband's arrow thrust into the ground, the speared crab, the broken twig, filled with tears.

"He orders that Iracema walk backwards like the crab, and keep him in her memory, as the passion-flower keeps its blossoms always until it dies."

The daughter of the Tabajaras slowly retraced her steps, without turning around, without taking her eyes from her husband's arrow; then she returned to the hut. Sitting there in the threshold with her head on her knees, she waited, until sleep calmed the pain in her breast.

As soon as day had dawned, she went with swift steps toward the lake, and arrived at its edge. The arrow was there as it had been the evening before: her husband had not returned.

Since then, at the hour of the bath, instead of going to the lake of beauty, where in earlier days she had taken such pleasure in swimming, she would go to the other one, which had witnessed her husband's abandonment. She would sit beside the arrow until night fell; then she would return to the hut.

As swiftly as she went out in the morning, just as slowly would she return in the evening. The same warriors who had seen her joyful in the waters of the Porangaba, now finding her melancholy and alone, like the widowed heron on the riverbank, called that place Mecejana,[1] which meant the abandoned one.

Once, when Araquém's beautiful daughter lamented beside the lake of Mecejana, a strident voice called her name from the heights of a carnauba tree:

"Iracema! . . . Iracema! . . ."

She raised her eyes and saw among the leaves of a palm her lovely *jandaia*, beating its wings and ruffling its feathers at the pleasure of seeing her.

The memory of her homeland, effaced by love, surged once more in her thought. She saw the beautiful fields of Ipu, the slopes of the sierra where she was born, Araquém's hut, and felt longing; but even at that instant she did not regret having abandoned them.

Its mouth twittered a song. Spreading its wings, the *jandaia* fluttered about and perched on her shoulder. Lovingly extending its neck, with its black beak it smoothed her hair and pecked at her mouth, as delicate and red as the cherry.

Iracema recalled that she had been ungrateful with her *jandaia*, forgetting it in times of happiness; but the *jandaia* came to console her now in her time of misfortune.

That evening she did not return alone to the hut. During the day her nimble fingers wove a beautiful cage of straw, which she lined with the soft down of the *monguba*[2] tree to house her companion and friend.

The following dawn, it was the *jandaia*'s voice that awakened her. The lovely bird never again left its mistress, either because after the long absence it could not see its fill of her or because it sensed that she had need of company in her melancholy sorrow.

XXVII

One evening Iracema saw in the distance two warriors approaching along the seashore. Her heart beat more quickly.

An instant later, she was forgetting in her husband's arms the many days of longing and abandonment that she had spent in the lonely hut.

Martim and his brother had arrived at Jacaúna's village when the war trumpet sounded: they had led into battle Poti's thousand bows. Once again the Tabajaras, despite their alliance with the white barbarians of the Mearim, had been vanquished by the valiant Pitiguaras.

Never was a victory more disputed or a combat more hotly contested than that fought in the lands watered by the Acaracu and the Camucim; valor was equal on both sides, and neither of the two peoples would have been defeated had not grim Arequi, the god of war, decided to give these shores to the race of the white warrior, the allies of the Pitiguara.

Soon after the victory the Christian had returned to the beaches of the sea, where he had built a hut and where his tender wife awaited him. Again, he felt in his soul the thirst for love, and he trembled at the thought that Iracema might have gone, leaving uninhabited that site once so full of happiness.

As the dry prairie, at the coming of winter turns green again and arrays itself in flowers, the beautiful daughter of the interior, with the return of her husband, took on new life; and her beauty embellished itself with soft and tender smiles.

Her grace once again filled the Christian's eyes, and happiness came to dwell anew in her heart.

The Christian loved the daughter of the interior as in the first days, when it seems that time will never have any power to stay the heart. But only a few days served to wither those flowers of a soul exiled from its homeland.

The mombin, child of the sierra, if it grows in the plains because wind or birds have borne its seed, flourishes when it finds good soil and cool shade; perhaps its green foliage may one day form a crown and bear flower. But one gust from the sea is enough to wither everything. Its leaves bestrew the ground, and the wind carries away its blooms.

Like the mombin[1] of the plains, so was the heart of the white warrior in that savage land. Friendship and love accompanied and strengthened him for a time, but now, far from home and from his brothers, he felt he was in the wilderness. His friend and his wife were no longer enough for his being, filled with great desires and noble ambitions.

He would spend the days, once so brief, now long, on the beach, hearing the wailing of the wind and the sobbing of the waves. With eyes engulfed in the immensity of the horizon, he sought, to no avail, to discover in the diaphanous blue the whiteness of a sail lost on the seas.

Far from the hut, there rose beside the ocean a tall hill of sand; from its resemblance to the crocodile's head the fishermen called it Jacarecanga.[2] From the heart of the white sands scorched by the blazing sun flowed pure, cool water. And it is thus that the soul distills from the heart of pain sweet tears of relief and consolation.

The Christian would climb that mound; and there remain, contemplating his fate. Sometimes the thought came to his mind of returning to his land and his own; but he knew that Iracema would go with him, and that memory tortured his heart. Every step that took the daughter of the Tabajaras farther from her native lands, now that she no longer had the nest of his heart to shelter her, was a portion of life that he stole from her.

Poti recognized that Martim wished to be alone, and discreetly withdrew. The warrior knew what troubled the soul of his brother; and he expected everything of time, for time alone hardens the warrior's heart, like the heartwood of the jacaranda.

Iracema also avoided her husband's eyes, for she had come to know that those beloved eyes were troubled at the sight of her, and instead of filling themselves with her beauty as before, dismissed it from themselves. But her eyes did not weary of accompanying, secretly and from afar, the warrior her master, who had made captives of them.

Woe to the wife! . . . She felt the blow in her heart, and like the copaiba tree wounded in its core, her tears flowed in an unbroken stream.

XXVIII

O ne day, the Christian heard in his soul the sob-
bing of Iracema: his eyes looked about him but
did not see her.

Araquém's daughter was off among the verdant *ubaia*
thickets, sitting on the greensward. Tears streamed
from her lovely face, and the drops that tumbled one by
one fell onto her bosom, where the child of love was al-
ready throbbing and growing. In this way fall the leaves
of the luxuriant tree before the ripening of the fruit.

"What is it that squeezes tears from Iracema's
heart?"

"The cashew tree weeps when it becomes a sad and
lifeless trunk. Iracema has lost her happiness since you
separated from her."

"Am I not here beside you?"

"Your body is here, but your soul flies to the land of
your fathers, and it seeks the white virgin who awaits
you."

Martim felt pain. The large dark eyes that the Indian woman had turned to him had wounded him in the depths of his being.

"The white warrior is your husband; he belongs to you."

The beautiful Tabajara woman smiled in her sorrow: "How long ago did you withdraw your spirit from Iracema? In earlier days, your footstep would guide you to the cool sierras and the joyful plains: your feet would take delight in treading the land of happiness and would follow the track of your wife. Now you seek nothing but the burning ocean shores, because the sea that murmurs there comes from the lands where you were born, and the hill of sand, because from its top can be spied the boat that passes by."

"It is the desire to fight the Tupinambá that turns the warrior's steps to the edge of the sea," replied the Christian.

Iracema continued: "Your lips have become barren for your wife; so too does the sugarcane, when the long sunny days blaze, lose its honey, and its withered leaves no longer sing in the passing breeze. Now you speak only to the wind of the shore, so that it may carry your voice to the hut of your fathers."

"The white warrior's voice calls his brothers to defend the hut of Iracema and the land of his child, when the enemy comes."

His wife shook her head: "When you walk in the plains, your eyes flee from the fruit of the genipap and seek out the flower of the bramble. The fruit is delicious, but it has the color of the Tabajaras; the flower has the color of the white virgin's cheeks. If the birds sing, your ears no longer enjoy the *graúna's* sweet song, but your soul opens to the cry of the *japim*,[1] because it has golden feathers like the hair of the one you love!"

"Sadness darkens Iracema's eyes and embitters her lips. But happiness will return to his wife's heart, as the green branch returns to the tree."

"When your child is born, Iracema will die, like rice after it has given its fruit. Then the white warrior will have nothing more to bind him to the foreign land."

"Your voice, daughter of Araquém, burns like the wind from the interior of Icó at the time of the great heat. Would you abandon your husband?"

"Do your eyes not see the shapely jacaranda that rises to the heavens? At its feet lies the dry root of the leafy myrtle, which each winter covered itself in branches and red berries, to embrace its brother trunk. If it did not die, the jacaranda would not have the sunlight to grow so tall. Iracema is the dark leaf[2] that shades your soul; she must fall, so that joy may illuminate your heart."

The Christian embraced the body of the beautiful Indian and clasped her to his breast. His lips touched his wife's lips with a kiss, but severely and without warmth.

XXIX

Poti returned from his bath. He followed in the sand the tracks of Coatiabo and climbed to the top of Jacarecanga. There he found the warrior standing at the summit of the mount, with his eyes far off and his arms extended toward the broad seas.

The Pitiguara turned his gaze and spied a *maracatim* plowing the green waters, driven by the wind: "Is it the great boat of the brothers of my brother who come in search of him?"

The Christian sighed: "They are the white warriors who are the enemies of my race, seeking the shores of the valiant Pitiguara nation for their war of vengeance: they were vanquished along with the Tabajaras on the banks of the Camucim; now they come with their friends, the Tupinambás,[1] by the path of the sea."

"My brother is a great chieftain. What does he think his brother Poti should do?"

"Call the hunters of Soipé and the fishermen of the Trairi. We will go to meet with them."

Poti awakened the voice of the war trumpet, and the two warriors departed for the Mocoripe. Soon afterward they saw the warriors of Jaguaraçu and Camoropim hastening to the cry of war. Jacaúna's brother told them of the coming of the enemy.

The large boat cut swiftly through the waves along the land that extends to the banks of the Parnaíba. The moon was beginning to wax when it left the waters of the Mearim; contrary winds had driven it out to sea, far from its destination.

The Pitiguara warriors, in order not to drive away the enemy, hid among the cashew trees and followed the large boat along the beach. During the day they spied its white sails; at night, its fires crossed the blackness of the sea like fireflies lost in the forest.

For many suns they marched in this fashion. They passed the Camucim and finally trod the beautiful banks of the bay of parrots.[2]

Poti sent a warrior to great Jacaúna and prepared for combat. Martim, who mounted the hill of sand, knew that the *maracatim*[3] would seek shelter in a bay, and so advised his brother.

The sun had already risen; the yellow-haired warriors and the Tupinambás, their friends, flew over the waves in their light dugout canoes and disembarked on the beach. They formed a large arc and advanced like a school of fish when it cleaves the river's current.

In the center were the warriors of fire, who brought the thunderbolt; on the flanks, the warriors from the Mearim, who brandished their clubs.

But no nation ever wielded the well-aimed bow like the mighty Pitiguara nation; and Poti was the greatest chieftain of all the chieftains who ever took to hand the war trumpet. Beside him strode his brother, as great a chief as he, and versed in the cunning of the white race with yellow hair.

During the night the Pitiguaras drove into the beach a strong *caiçara*[4] of thorns, and raised before it a wall of sand against which the thunderbolt cools and loses its strength. There, they awaited the enemy. Martim ordered other warriors to the top of the highest coconut trees; there, protected by the large fronds, they awaited the moment of combat.

Poti's was the first arrow launched, and the leader of the yellow-hairs was the first warrior to bite the dust in the foreign land. The thunderbolts roared in the hands of the white warriors, but the bolts they discharged lodged in the sand, or went astray in the air.

The arrows of the Pitiguaras now rained from the sky, now flew up from the earth, and all buried themselves in the enemy's breast. Each warrior fell riddled with many shafts, like the prey disputed by piranhas in the waters of the lake.

The enemies embarked again in their pirogues and returned to the great vessel for the large, heavy thunder-makers that no man alone, or even two, could manage.

As they were returning, the chieftain of the fishermen, who swam in the water like the fleet shrimp from which he took his name, dived into the waves. Before the foam had settled, the enemy pirogue had sunk as if swallowed by a whale.

Night came, and with it, peace.

At break of day, the large craft was fleeing on the horizon for the banks of the Mearim. Jacaúna arrived, no longer for combat but for the feast of victory.

At the time that the Pitiguara warriors' song celebrated the defeat of the *guaraciabas*, the yellow-haired foreigners, the first child that the blood of the white race had begotten in this land of freedom saw the light in the plains of Porangaba.

XXX

Iracema, feeling that her womb was bursting, sought out the riverbank where the coconut tree grew.

She gripped the trunk of the palm. Pain lacerated her viscera, but soon an infant's cry flooded her soul with jubilation.

The young mother, gratified at such good fortune, took the tender child in her arms and with him plunged into the limpid waters of the river. Then she held him to her delicate breast; her eyes enfolded him in sadness and love.

"You are Moacir,[1] the child born of my suffering."

The *jandaia*, sitting at the crest of the palm tree, repeated "Moacir," and from then on, in its song the companionable bird joined to the name of the mother the name of her child.

The innocent child slept; Iracema sighed: "The bee makes its honey in the fragrant trunk of the sassafras; during all the season of flowers it flies from branch to branch, collecting the nectar to fill the combs; but it never tastes its sweetness, because the tayra devours in a single night the entire hive. Your mother, too, son of my anguish, will not drink from your lips the honey of your smile."

The young mother placed on her shoulders the wide swath of soft cotton that she had made to carry her son always next to her hip, and she followed through the sand the trail of her husband, who had departed three days before. She walked gently lest she wake the baby, sleeping like a tiny bird under the maternal wing.

When she came to the great hill of sand, she saw that the trail of Martim and Poti continued along the beach, and she guessed that they were gone to war. Her heart sighed, but her dry eyes sought the countenance of her son.

She turned her face to the Mocoripe: "Thou art the hill of joy, but for Iracema thou holdest only sorrow."

Upon her return, the new mother placed the sleeping child in his father's hammock, bereft and solitary in the middle of the hut, and lay on the ground, on the mat where she had slept ever since her husband's arms had no longer opened to receive her.

The light of morning was entering the hut, and with it Iracema saw the shadow of a warrior enter.

At the door stood Caubi.

Martim's wife sprang up and rushed forward to protect her son. Her brother raised his sad eyes from the hammock to her and spoke in an even sadder voice: "It was not vengeance that tore Caubi from the land of the Tabajaras; he has already forgiven you. It was the desire to see Iracema, who took with her all his happiness."

"Then welcome is the warrior Caubi to the hut of his brother," responded Iracema, embracing him.

"The one born of your womb sleeps in that hammock; Caubi's eyes would gladly look upon him."

Iracema opened the fringe of feathers and showed the child's lovely countenance. After contemplating him for a long time, Caubi said, smiling, "He has nursed upon your soul."[2]

And he kissed in the young mother's eyes the image of the child, whom he made no move to touch, fearful of doing it harm.

The daughter's tremulous voice echoed: "Does Araquém still walk the earth?"

"He still grieves; after you left him, his head drooped upon his chest and has not been raised again."

"You must tell him that Iracema has died, so that he may find consolation."

Caubi's sister prepared a meal for the warrior and strung on the porch the hammock of hospitality for him to rest from the weariness of the journey. When the traveler had satisfied his appetite, he rose with these words: "Tell me where your husband my brother is, so the warrior Caubi can give him the embrace of friendship."

The sighing lips of the unhappy wife moved, like the breeze-ruffled petals of the cactus flower, then said nothing. But her eyes dissolved into tears, which fell like beads.

Caubi's face clouded: "Your brother thought that unhappiness had remained in the lands you abandoned, because you brought with you all the laughter of those who loved you!"

Iracema dried her eyes: "The husband of Iracema departed with the warrior Poti to the beaches of the Acaracu. Before three suns have illuminated the earth he will return, and with him the happiness to his wife's soul."

"The warrior Caubi will await him to learn what he has done with the smile that dwelled on your lips."

The Tabajara brave's voice had grown hoarse; his restive steps paced aimlessly about the hut.

XXXI

Iracema was singing softly, rocking the hammock to lull her son to sleep.

The sand of the beach crackled under the strong, firm feet of the Tabajara warrior returning from the seaside after his abundant catch of fish.

The young mother overlapped the fringes of the hammock so that the flies could not disturb the sleeping child, and went to greet her brother: "Caubi must return to the mountains of the Tabajaras!" she said softly.

The warrior's face saddened: "You send your brother from the hut so that he will not see the sorrow that dwells in it."

"Araquém had many children in his youth; some were carried off by war and died like braves; others took a wife and engendered in turn numerous offspring; the children of Araquém's old age are but two. Iracema is the dove that the hunter took from its nest. There remains only Caubi for the old pajé, to sustain his stooped body and guide his trembling step."

"Caubi will depart when the shadow has left Iracema's face."

"Like the star that shines only at night, Iracema lives in her sorrow. Only her husband's eyes can erase the shadow from her face. Go, so that they may not lose their brilliance at the sight of you."

"Your brother departs to satisfy your will, but he will return each time the cashew tree flowers, to feel in his heart the child of your womb."

He went into the hut. Iracema took the child from the hammock; and both, mother and son, trembled against the Tabajara warrior's chest. Then Caubi went to the door and disappeared among the trees.

Iracema, her tremulous steps dragging, followed him from afar until he was lost from sight at the edge of the forest. There she stopped: when the *jandaia*'s cry, mixed with the infant's wail, called her back to the hut, her secret tears had been absorbed by the fine sand where she had sat.

The young mother held the child to her nipple, but the infant's mouth did not fall silent. Her sparse milk did not swell her breast.

The unhappy woman's blood had been thinned by the unending tears that flowed relentlessly from her eyes; little made its way to her breasts, where the first liquor of life is formed.

She dissolved white *carimã*[1] and prepared over the fire the porridge to feed her son. When the sun turned golden the tips of the hills, she left for the forest, carrying at her bosom the sleeping child.

In the thickness of the wood was the den of the absent tayra. The young pups were grunting and rolling over each other. The beautiful Tabajara approached quietly. She prepared her son a cradle from the soft branches of the granadilla and sat down nearby.

One by one, she placed the tayra pups in her lap and yielded to them her delicate breasts, whose cherry-red nipples she anointed with honey. The ravenous pups sucked her breasts, greedy for milk.

Iracema suffered pain unlike any she had ever felt. They seemed to be draining away her life; but her breasts began to fill. At last they swelled, and the milk, still red from the blood from which it was formed, began to spurt.

The joyful mother cast from her the little pups, and, filled with jubilation, satisfied her child's hunger. Now was he doubly the child of her pain, both born and nourished from her.

Araquém's daughter felt at last that her veins were stanching their flow; yet her lips, bitter with sorrow, refused the food that might restore her strength. Lamentation and sighs had taken away the smile and the grace from her lovely mouth.

XXXII

The sun sank. Japi came from the woods and ran to the door of the hut.

Iracema, sitting with her child on her lap, was bathing in the rays of the sun and felt her body shiver from the cold. Seeing the animal, her husband's faithful messenger, hope revived her heart; she tried to rise to meet her warrior master, but her weakened limbs refused her will.

She fell, fainting, against the stay of the hut. Japi licked her cold hand and jumped playfully to make the child smile, with gentle yaps of pleasure. From time to time he would run to the edge of the woods and bark, calling his master, then return to the hut to display his happiness to the mother and child.

At that time, Martim was treading the yellow fields of the Tauape;[1] his brother Poti, inseparable, walked beside him.

Eight moons had passed since he had left the

beaches of Jacarecanga. With the defeat of the yellow-haired foe, at the bay of parrots, the Christian warrior had departed for the banks of the Mearim, where dwelled the barbarian ally of the Tupinambás.

Poti and his warriors had accompanied him. After they had crossed the rushing arm of the sea that comes from the sierra of Tauatinga and bathes the plains where *piau*,[2] minnows, are caught, they had spied at last the shores of the Mearim, and the old village[3] of the barbarian enemy.

More and more, the yellow-haired race was winning the friendship of the Tupinambás; the number of white warriors, who had built on the island a large *itaoca*[4] from which to discharge their lightning, was growing.

When Martim had seen what he desired, he had returned to the lands of the Porangaba, which he now trod. He heard the rumble of the sea on the beaches of the Mocoripe; the breath of the ocean waves blew against his face.

The closer his steps brought him to the hut, the slower and heavier they became. He was fearful of arriving, and he felt that his soul would suffer when into it penetrated the sorrowful, aggrieved eyes of his wife.

Words had long ago deserted his dry lips; his friend respected his silence, which he well understood. It was the silence of the river when it passes through deep and lowering places.

As soon as the two warriors trod upon the river-banks, they heard the dog's bark calling them and the *jandaia*'s cry of lamentation. They were near the hut, which was hidden only by a spit of forest. The Christian halted, pressing his hand to his chest to restrain his heart, which leapt like the eel.

"Japi's bark is one of joy," said the chieftain.

"Because he has arrived; but the *jandaia*'s voice is one of sorrow. Will the absent warrior find peace in the soul of his lonely wife, or will longing have killed in her the fruit of love?"

The Christian advanced his hesitant step. Suddenly, between the tree boughs, his eyes beheld, sitting at the door of the hut, Iracema with her child on her lap, and the dog cavorting about. His heart thrust him forward with a bound, and his soul burst forth from his lips: "Iracema! . . ."

The sorrowing wife and mother half-opened her eyes upon hearing the beloved voice. With great effort, she raised the child in her arms and presented him to his father, who looked at him ecstatically in his love.

"Receive the child of your blood. In good time; no longer can my barren breasts feed him!"

Placing the child in his father's arms, the unhappy mother lost her vitality, like the sweet potato when its bulb is uprooted. Her husband saw then how pain had consumed her lovely body; but the beauty yet dwelled there, like the perfume in the fallen *manacá* [5] flower.

Iracema did not rise again from the hammock where Martim's distressed arms placed her. The gentle husband, in whom love had been reborn with paternal joy, surrounded her with caresses that filled her soul with happiness, but could not bring her back to life: the stamen of her flower had been broken.

"Bury the body of your wife beneath the coconut tree that you so loved. When the wind from the sea blows among its leaves, Iracema will think it is your voice rustling through her hair."

The gentle lips fell silent forever; the final light flickered from her lusterless eyes.

Poti sustained his brother in his great sorrow. Martim understood how precious is a true friend in time of misfortune: he is like the hillock that shelters from the gale the strong, sturdy trunk of the ironwood when the *cupim* [6] bores into its essence.

The *camucim* that received Iracema's body, steeped in fragrant resins, was buried beneath the coconut tree, at the edge of the river. Martim broke off a myrtle branch, the leaf of sorrow, and placed it on his wife's grave.

The *jandaia*, perched atop the palm, repeated sadly, "Iracema!"

From that time, the Pitiguara warriors who passed by the abandoned hut and heard the plaintive voice of the companionate bird withdrew, their souls filled with sorrow, from the coconut tree where the *jandaia* sang.

And thus it was that one day the river where the coconut grew, and the lands where the river meanders, came to be called Ceará.

XXXIII

Four times the cashew flowered after Martim departed from the shores of Ceará, taking on the fragile boat his son and the faithful dog. The *jandaia* had refused to leave the land where its friend and mistress slept.

The first child born in Ceará, still in his cradle, had left his homeland. Did this presage the destiny of a race?

Poti built the village of his warriors on the bank of the river and awaited the brother who had promised to return. Every morning he climbed the hill of sand to turn his eyes to the ocean to see if the whiteness of a friendly sail appeared in the distance.

Martim returned at last to the lands that had been his happiness and were now his bitter longing. When his feet felt the warmth of the white sands, there pervaded his being a fire that burned his heart: it was the flame of the memories that flared like the spark beneath ashes.

That flame was not appeased until he stood on the earth where his wife slept; for in that instant, his heart suffused, like the courbaril in the burning heat, and with copious tears bedewed his sorrow.

Many warriors of his race accompanied the white chieftain, to found with him the Christians' city. A priest of their religion came also, garbed in black, to plant the cross in the savage land.

Poti was the first to kneel at the foot of the sacred wood; he would allow nothing more to separate him from his white brother. Both must have a single god, as they shared a single heart.

As his baptismal name he received that of the saint whose day it was, and that of the king whom he was to serve, followed by his own, in the language of his new brothers. His fame grew, and even today he is the pride of the land where first he saw the light.

The city that Martim had erected on the bank of the river, on the shores of the Ceará, flourished. The word of the true God germinated in the savage land, and the holy bells echoed in the valleys where the gourd rattle once sounded.

Jacaúna came to live in the fields of the Porangaba to be close to his white friend; Camarão had built his warriors' village on the banks of the Mecejana.

Some time later, when Albuquerque,[1] the great leader of the white warriors, came, Martim and Camarão departed for the banks of the Mearim to wreak punishment upon the fierce Tupinambás and expel the white barbarian enemy.

It was always with emotion that the husband of Iracema gazed again upon the country where he had been so happy, and the green leaves under whose shade slept the beautiful Tabajara woman.

He would often go to sit on those gentle sands, to meditate and soothe the bitter longing in his breast.

From the crest of the coconut palm, the *jandaia* still sang; but no longer did it repeat the melodious name of Iracema.

On earth, all things pass away.

Notes

Historical argument—In 1603, Pero Coelho, a nobleman from Paraíba, set out as military commander on a mission of discovery, taking with him a force of eighty colonists and eight hundred Indians. He arrived at Jaguaribe Falls and founded there the settlement given the name of Nova Lisboa. This was the first colonial establishment in Ceará.

When Pero Coelho was abandoned by his partners, João Soromenho was sent with help. This officer, authorized to take captives to offset expenses, failed to respect even Jaguaribe Indians, friends of the Portuguese.

This led to the downfall of the nascent settlement. The colonists withdrew because of the hostility of the indigenous population, and Pero Coelho, deserted, was forced to return to Paraíba by land, with his wife and young children.

On the first expeditions was a young man from Rio Grande do Norte named Martim Soares Moreno, who formed a friendship with Jacaúna, chieftain of the Indians of the coast, and his brother Poti. In 1608, by order of Diogo de Meneses, he returned to initiate systematic colonization in that captaincy, which he did, founding the garrisoned fort of Nossa Senhora do Amparo in 1611.

Jacaúna, who lived on the banks of the Acaracu, settled with his tribe in the vicinity of the new settlement, to protect it against the Indians of the interior and the French, who were to be found in great number on the coast.

Poti received the baptismal name of Antônio Filipe Camarão, a name he glorified in the war against the Dutch. His services were rewarded with a grant of nobility, the Commendation of Christ, and the post of military commander of the Indians.

Martin Soares Moreno became a lieutenant general and was one of the fine Portuguese commanding officers who freed Brazil from the Dutch invasion. Ceará should honor his memory as that of an outstanding man and its true founder, as the first settlement at the falls of the Jaguaribe River was a mere frustrated attempt.

This is the historical argument of the legend; other contributions received from the chroniclers of the time will be indicated in special notes.

There is a historical question relevant to this matter: I speak of the homeland of Camarão, about which one writer from Pernambuco has tried to raise doubts, taking Ceará's glory to give it to his own province.

This point, which has been contested only in modern times by Sr. Comendador Melo in his *Biographies*, strikes me as sufficiently elucidated, after the erudite letter from Sr. Basílio Quaresma Torreão published in the *Mercantil*, no. 26, of January 26, 1860, page 2.

However, I must insist upon an observation.

In the first place, the oral tradition is an important historical source, sometimes the purest and truest. Now, in the province of Ceará, in Sobral, not only was information about Camarão alluded to among the common folk, but there was also an old woman who claimed to be his niece. This tradition was collected by various writers, among them the well-known author of the *Corografia Brasílica*.

The author of *Valeroso Lucideno* is among the older writers the only one who states that Camarão is a son of Pernambuco; but in addition to disputing this assertion, the version of other writers of note adds that Berredo explains perfectly the dictum of that writer when he speaks of Pero Coelho's expedition to Jaguaribe, *a site at that time and still today under the jurisdiction of Pernambuco.*

It is necessary to clarify another point lest I be censured as unfaithful to historical truth. That is the nation to which Jacaúna and Camarão belonged, which some hold to be the Tabajara.

There is a manifest error in this.

All the chronicles speak of the tribes of Jacaúna and Camarão as inhabitants of the coast, and as such they aided in the founding of Ceará, as they had earlier aided in the founding of Nova Lisboa in Jaguaribe. Now, the nation that inhabited the coast between the Parnaíba and the Jaguaribe or Rio Grande was the Pitiguaras, as Gabriel Soares attests. The Tabajaras inhabited the mountain range of Ibiapaba, and therefore the interior.

As chieftains of the Tabajaras are mentioned Mel-Redondo in Ceará and Grão Deabo in Piauí. These chieftains were always irreconcilable and hateful enemies of the Portuguese and allies of the French in Maranhão, who penetrated as far as Ibiapaba. Jacaúna and Camarão are known for their firm alliance with the Portuguese.

But what settles the issue is the following text. It is found in the *Memórias diárias* of the Brazilian wars by the Count of Pernambuco:

"1634, January 18: Because of the good conduct with which A. F. Camarão has served, the King has made him commander of all the Indians not only *of his nation, which was the Pitiguar,* but of all the other dwellers in the several villages."

This authority, in addition to being contemporaneous and the word of a witness, cannot be rejected, especially when it expresses itself so positively and intentionally about the matter in dispute.

I

1. *Onde canta a jandaia*—Tradition says that Ceará means in the indigenous language "song of the jandaia."

Aires do Casal, in *Corografia Brasílica,* refers to this tradition. Senator Pompeu, in his excellent topographic dictionary, mentions an opinion, new to me, that views *Siará* as coming from the word *suia*, "hunt," in virtue of the abundance of game found on the banks of the river. This etymology is forced. To designate quantity, the Tupi language used the suffix *iba*; the suffix *ára* attached to verbs designates the subject exercising the present action; attached to nouns, what the object presently has. Examples: *Coatiara*, "he who paints," *Juçara*, "that which has thorns."

Ceará is a noun composed of *cemo*, "sing loudly, shout," and *ára*, "small macaw or parakeet." This is the true etymology; it conforms not only to tradition but to the rules of the Tupi language.

2. Iracema in Guarani means lips of honey—from *ira*, "honey," and *tembe*, "lips." Tembe in combination becomes *ceme*, as in the word *ceme iba*.

3. Jirau—On the raft is a kind of pallet where the passengers make themselves comfortable; sometimes it is covered with a straw roof. In general it is any kind of grating raised above ground level and supported from underneath.

II

1. Graúna—This the well-known bird of glossy black color. Its name comes from a corruption of *guira*, 'bird,' and *una*, abbreviation of *pixuna*, "black."

2. Jati—A small bee that produces delicious honey.

3. Ipu—A certain type of very fertile land, which forms great rises or islands amid the tablelands and the interior and is highly sought after for cultivation, is even today known by this name in Ceará. From it derives the name of that district of the province.

4. Tabajara—Lord of the villages, from *taba*, "village," and *jara*, "lord." This nation dominated the interior of the province, especially the Ibiapaba mountain range.

5. Oiticica—A leafy tree appreciated for the delightful cool cast by its shade.

6. Gará—A marsh bird, widely known by the name of *guará*. I believe that this name is a corruption of its true origin, which is *ig*, "water," and *ará*, "macaw": water macaw, so-called for its beautiful red color.

7. Ará—Parakeet. The natives repeated as an augmentative the final syllable of a word and sometimes the entire word, as in *murémuré*: *muré*, "flute," *murémuré*, "large flute." *Arárá* thus

came to be the augmentative of *ará* and would signify the larger species of the genus.

8. Uru—A small basket which served as the savages' coffer to store objects of greater price and esteem.

9. Crautá—A common bromeliad from which are taken fibers as fine as or finer than those of linen.

10. Juçara—A palm with large thorns, which are used even today to separate lace threads.

11. Uiraçaba—Case for arrows, from *uira*, "arrow," and the suffix *çaba*, "thing pertaining to."

12. Breaking the arrow—Among the Indians this was the symbolic means of establishing peace among the various tribes, or even between two warring enemies. We should warn from the outset not to find strange the manner in which the foreigner expresses himself in speaking with the Indians; his perfect knowledge of the Indians' customs and language, and especially his having conformed to them to the point of abandoning European clothing and painting himself, Martim Soares Moreno owed to the influences acquired among the Indians of Ceará.

III

1. Ibiapaba—A great mountain range that extends to the north of the province and separates it from Piauí. It means trimmed land. Dr. Martius in his *Glossário* attributes another etymology to it. *Iby*, "land," and *pabe*, "all." The former, however, has the authority of Vieira.

2. Igaçaba—Vase, pot, from *ig*, "water," and the suffix *çaba*, "thing pertaining to."

3. Have you come?—A common greeting of hospitality was *Ere iobê?* "Have you come?" *Pa-aiotu*—"Yes, I have come." *Auge-be*, "well said."

4. Jaguaribe—The largest river in the province; it took its name from the number of jaguars that populated its banks. *Jaguar*—a large spotted feline; *iba*—suffix to express great quantity, abundance.

5. Pitiguaras—The great nation of Indians who inhabited the shore of the province and extended from the Parnaíba to the Rio Grande do Norte. The orthography of the name is

quite corrupted in different versions, which has made it difficult to discover its etymology. *Iby* meant land; *iby-tira* came to signify sierra or high land. The indigenous peoples called the valleys *iby-tira-cua*, "girdle of the mountains." The suffix *jara*, "master," when augmented formed the word Ibiticuara, which by corruption gave Pitiguara, "lords of the valleys."

6. Martim—From the Latin origin of his name, which derives from Mars, the foreigner deduces the meaning that he gives to it.

7. Acaracu—The name of the river comes from *acará*, "heron," *co*, "hole, den, nest," and *y*, a doubtful sound between *i* and *u* that the Portuguese expressed now one way, now another, signifying water. River of the herons' nest is, therefore, the translation of *Acaracu*.

8. Evil spirit of the forest—The indigenous peoples called those spirits *caa-pora*, "inhabitants of the woods," from which by corruption came the word *caipora*, introduced into the Portuguese language in a figurative sense.

IV

1. The most beautiful women—This custom of hospitality in the Americas is attested to by the chroniclers. To it is attributed the noble and virtuous gesture of Anchieta, who, to strengthen his chastity, composed on the beaches of Iperoig the poem "The Virginity of Mary," the verses of which he would write in the wet sands to polish them.

2. Jurema—A tree of average size and dense foliage; it gives an extremely bitter fruit with an acrid odor, from which along with the leaves and other ingredients the savages prepared a drink that had the effect of hashish, producing dreams so vivid and intense that the person experienced with delight, and as if they were reality, the pleasant fantasies aroused by the narcotic. The manufacture of the liquor was a secret, exploited by the pajés in furtherance of their influence. *Jurema* is composed of *ju*, "thorn," and *rema*, "unpleasant smell."

3. Irapuã—From *ira*, "honey," and *apuam*, "round"; this is the name given to a virulent and irascible bee because of the round shape of its hive. By corruption, the name has been reduced to *arapuá*. The warrior dealt with here is the celebrated

Round-Honey, chieftain of the Tabajaras of the Ibiapaba mountain range, a bloodthirsty enemy of the Portuguese and friend of the French.

4. Unmoving star—The pole star, because of its immobility; the savages oriented themselves by it at night.

5. Boicininga—This is the rattlesnake, from *bóia*, "snake," and cininga, "rattle."

6. Oitibó—A nocturnal bird, a species of owl. Others say *noitibó*.

V

1. Spirit of darkness—The savages called these spirits *curupira*, "bad children," from *curumim*, "child," and *pira*, "bad."

2. Boré—Bamboo flute, the same as muré.

3. Ocara—A circular area in the middle of the village, surrounded by the stockade, onto which all the houses opened. Composed of *oca*, "house," and the suffix *ara*, "which has": that which has the house, or where the house is.

4. Potiguara—Shrimp eater; from *poty* and *uara*. Pejorative name given by their enemies to the Pitiguara, who inhabited the shores and lived in great part on fishing. This name is also used by some writers because they received it from their enemies.

5. Pocema—A great clamor made by the savages on joyous occasions; it is a word adopted in Portuguese and included in the Morais dictionary. It comes from *po*, "hand," and *cemo*, "to clamor": clamor of hands, because the savages accompanied the shouting with the clapping of hands and the thumping of weapons.

6. Andira—Bat; it is in allusion to his name that Irapuã later directs words of disdain at the aged warrior.

VI

1. Aracati—This noun means good weather; from *ara* and *catu*. The savages of the interior called by this name the sea breezes that normally blow at the end of the afternoon and, running through the valley of the Jaguaribe, spread through the countryside and provide relief from the blazing summer calm. From this fact the place from which this favorable wind blew came to be called *Aracati*. In Icó, the name is preserved even today for the afternoon breeze that blows from the sea.

VII

1. Aflar—In regard to this word, the following note was in the first edition: "About this verb that I introduced into the Portuguese language from the Latin *afflo*, I have already written my understanding of it in a note to the second edition of *Diva*, which will soon be published." This was a total mistake on my part, for the verb was used by Mousinho and Father Bernardes.

2. Anhanga—This is the name given the spirit of evil by the indigenous peoples; it is composed of *anho*, "alone," and *anga*, "soul": spirit alone, deprived of a body, ghost.

VIII

1. Camucim—A vessel in which the indigenous peoples buried the bodies of the dead and which served as their tombs; others say *camotim*, and perhaps with better orthography, because, if I am not mistaken, the name is a corruption of the phrase *co*, "hole," *ambira*, "deceased," and *anhotim*, "to bury": hole to bury the dead, or *c' am' otim*. The name was also given to any pot.

2. Andiroba—A tree that yields a bitter oil.

3. Hair the color of the sun—In Tupi, *guaraciaba*. This is what the indigenous peoples called the Europeans who had blond hair.

4. Capoeira—Corruption of *caa-apuam-era*, which means island of the woods already once cut.

IX

1. Moquém—From the verb *mocáem*, "roast over the flame." This was the manner in which the indigenous peoples preserved meat to prevent it from rotting when they took it with them on a journey. In the huts they kept it in the smoker.

2. Master of the pathway—Thus the indigenous peoples designated a guide; from *py*, "road," and *guara*, "master."

3. This will be a sad day—The Tupi called the afternoon *caruca*, according to the dictionary. According to Jean de Léry [author of a sixteenth-century treatise on Brazil], *che caruc acy* means "I am sad." Which of these was the figurative use of the word? Did they take the image of sadness from the

shadow of afternoon, or the image of twilight from the darkening of the spirit?

4. Jurupari—Demon; from *juru*, "mouth," and *apara*, "twisted, crippled": the twisted mouth.

5. Ubaia—Well-known fruit of the species Eugenia. It means pleasant fruit, from *uba*, "fruit," and *aia*, "healthy."

X

1. Jandaia—This name, which is found written in several ways, *nhendaia*, *nhandaia*, and in altered form in all of them, is merely a qualitative adjective from the noun *ará*. It is derived from the words *nheng*, "to speak," *antan*, "rough," and *ara*, a verbal suffix expressing the agent: *nh' ant' ara*; with the *t* replaced by *d* and the *r* by *i*, it became *nhandaia*, from which *jandaia*, which translated as "cawing parakeet." From the song of this bird, as has been seen, comes the name Ceará, according to the etymology given it by tradition.

2. Inhuma—Nocturnal palamedean bird. The species spoken of here is *Palamedea chavaria*, which normally sings at midnight. I believe the better spelling to be *anhuma*, perhaps from *anho*, "alone," and *anum*, "well-known portentous bird." *Anum* would thus signify solitary, so-called because of some sort of similarity to its unpleasant cry.

3. War trumpet—The indigenous peoples, according to Léry, had some so large that the diameter of the opening measured many spans.

XI

1. Guará—Wild dog, Brazilian wolf. This word comes from the verb *u*, "to eat," from which is formed with the relative *g* and the suffix *ara* the verbal *g-u-ára*, "eating." The final long syllable is the postpositive *á*, which serves to give emphasis to the word: *g-u-ára-á* "really eating, voracious."

2. Jibóia—A well-known snake; from *gi*, "ax," and *bóia*, "snake." The name was taken from the manner in which the snake springs, similar to the blow of an ax. It can correctly be translated as lunging snake.

3. Sucuri—The gigantic serpent that inhabits large rivers and can swallow an ox. From *suu*, "animal," and *cury* or *curu*,

"snoring": snoring animal, because the sucuri's roar is in fact terrifying.

4. If it is blood and not honey you have in your veins—An allusion that old Andira makes to Irapuã's name, which, as was said, means "round honey."

5. Hear his thunder—This entire episode of the rumbling of the earth is a ruse that the pajés and priests of that savage nation used to dominate the imagination of the people through enchantment. The hut was situated on a cliff where an underground passage connected to the plain by a narrow opening; Araquém had carefully covered both openings with large stones to conceal the grotto from the warriors. On this occasion the lower opening was uncovered, and the pajé was aware of the fact; by uncovering the upper opening, air was piped through the spiral cavern with a frightening stridor; the effect is similar to the murmur of a conch shell held to the ear. The event is in fact a natural one; the appearance, however, is wondrous.

6. Maracá—An emblem of war; from *mará*, "combat," and *aca*, "horn, point." The maraca served as a standard for the Tupis.

7. Abati in the water—*Abati* is the Tupi noun for rice; Iracema makes use of the image of rice, which only thrives in flooded areas, to express her happiness.

XIV

1. Ubiratã—Ironwood; from *ubira*, "wood," and *antan*, "hard."

2. Maracajá—A wild cat with spotted skin.

3. Caititus—Wild pigs of the forest, a species of Brazilian peccary. From *caeté*, "wild and virgin woods," and *suu*, "hunt," by changing the *s* to *t* for euphony in the language.

4. Jaguar—We have seen that *guará* means voracious. Jaguar has unquestionably the same etymology; it is the verb form *guara* and the pronoun *já*, "us." The jaguar, therefore, was to the indigenous peoples all the animals that devoured them. *Jaguareté*—the great devourer.

5. Anajê—Sparrow hawk.

6. Acauã—A bird that preys upon snakes; from *caa*, "wood," and *uan*, from the verb *u*, "to eat." Aires do Casal says that its name comes from the cry it emits.

XV

1. Saí—A beautiful bird, of which there are several species, the most graceful being the *saixê*, for both its plumage and its song.

2. At the white maiden's waist—The indigenous peoples called the possessed lover *aguaçaba*, from *aba*, "man," *cua*, "waist," and *çaba*, "thing pertaining to": the woman that man encircles or brings to his waist. Iracema's thought is therefore clear.

3. Carioba—A cotton shirt; from *cary*, "white," and *oba*, "clothing." There was also *araçóia*, from *arara* and *aba*, "garment of parrot feathers."

XVI

1. Jaci—The moon. From the pronoun *ja*, "we," and *cy*, "mother." The moon denoted the month for the savages, and its birth was always celebrated by them.

2. Fires of joy—The savages called fires or torches *tory*; and *toryba*, "joy, feast, great quantity of torches."

3. Bucã—This signifies a type of grill that the savages made to roast the meat from the hunt; from it derives the French verb *boucaner*. The word comes from the Tupi or Guarani language.

XVII

1. Abaeté—Distinguished man; from *aba*, "man," and *etê*, "strong, illustrious."

XVIII

1. Jacaúna—Back jacaranda, from *jaca*, abbreviation of *jacarandá*, and *una*, "black." This Jacaúna is the celebrated chieftain and the friend of Martim Soares Moreno.

2. Cuandu—The porcupine.

3. War necklace—The necklace that the savages made from the teeth of their defeated enemies; it was both a coat of arms and a trophy of bravery.

XIX

1. Japi—It means "our foot," from the pronoun *ja*, "we," and *py*, "foot."

2. Ibiapina—From *iby*, "land," and *apino*, "to shear."

3. Jatobá—A large, regal tree. The scene is placed in what is today called Vila Viçosa, which tradition holds to be the birthplace of Camarão.

XX

1. Meruoca—From *meru*, "fly," and *oca*, "house." A mountain range near Sobral, fertile in foodstuffs.
2. Uruburetama—"Homeland or nest of vultures": a rather high sierra.
3. Mundaú—A very winding river that rises in the Uruburetama sierra. *Mundé*, "snare," and *hu*, "river."
4. Potengi—A river that waters the city of Natal, of which Soares Moreno was a son.

XXI

1. The savory traíra—This is the river Trairi, thirty leagues to the north of the capital. From *traíra*, "fish," and *y*, "river." Today it is a peaceful town and district.
2. Piroquara—From *pira*, "fish," and *coara*, "refuge."
3. Soipé—Country of the hunt. From *sôo*, "hunt," and *ipé*, "place where." Today it is called Siupé, the river and the town belonging to the parish and township of Fortaleza, situated on the bank of the marshlands called Jaguaruçu, at the mouth of the river.
4. Cauípe—From *cauim*, "cashew wine," and *ipe*, "place where."
5. River that forms an arm of the sea—This is the Parnaíba, a river in Piauí. It comes from *pará*, "sea," *nhanhe*, "run," and *hyba*, "arm": running arm of the sea. It is usually said that *pará* means river and *paraná* ocean; it is precisely the opposite.
6. Mocoripe—A hill of sand in the bay of the same name, one league distant from Fortaleza. It comes from *corib*, "to gladden," and *mo*, a particle or abbreviation of the verb *monhang*, "to make," which is joined to neutral and even active verbs to give them a passive meaning. For example, *caneon*, "to be distressed"; *mocaneon*, "to distress someone."
7. White tapuias—In Tupi, *tapuitanga*. A name the Pitiguaras gave the French to distinguish them from the Tupinambás. Tapuia also means "barbarian," "enemy." From *taba*, "village," and *puir*, "to flee": those who fled the village.

8. Mairi—City. It perhaps comes from the name of *mair*, "foreigner" and may have been applied to the settlements of whites as opposed to the Indians' villages.

XXII

1. Batuireté—The notable snipe; from *batuira* and *eté*. Nickname taken by the Pitiguara chieftain, which in figurative language had the meaning of brave swimmer. It is the name of an extremely fertile mountain range and the district that it occupies.

2. His stars were many—The indigenous peoples counted the years by the birth of the Pleiades in the East; they also had the custom of storing a nut for each season of the cashew, to mark their age.

3. Jatobá—A leafy tree, perhaps from *jetahy*, *oba*, "leaf," and *a*, augmentative: jetaí with a large crown. It is the name of a river and a sierra in Santa Quitéria.

4. Quixeramobim—According to Dr. Martius, it is translated by that expression of longing. It is composed of *Qui*, "ah!," *xere*, "my," and *amôbinhê*, "other times."

5. Path of the herons—In Tupi, Acarape, a settlement in the parish of Baturité, nine leagues from the capital.

6. Maranguab—The sierra of Maranguape, five leagues from the capital, is notable for its fertility and beauty. The indigenous name is composed of *maran*, "to wage war," and *couab*, "one who knows"; *maran* is perhaps an abbreviation of *maramonhang*, "to make war," if not, as I believe, the simple noun "war," from which the compound verb was formed. Dr. Martius adduces a different etymology: *mara*, "tree," *angai*, "in no way," *guabe*, "to eat."

This etymology does not appear to me as appropriate for the object, which is a mountain range, nor does it conform to the precepts of the language.

7. Pirapora—The Maranguape River, notable for the coolness of its waters and the excellence of the baths called Pirapora, at the site of the falls. It comes from the noun *pira*, "fish," and *pore*, "leap": leap of the fish.

8. The white hawk—Batuireté calls this the white warrior, while he calls his grandson "snipe"; he prophesies in this parallel the destruction of his race by the white race.

XXIII

1. Porangaba—It means "beauty." It is a lake one league from the city on a delightful site. Today it is called the Arronches; on its banks is the declining settlement of the same name.

2. Jereraú—River of the ducks; from *jerere* or *irerê*, "duck," and *hu*, "water." This place is notable even today for the excellence of its fruit, especially the beautiful oranges known as *Jereraú oranges*.

3. Sapiranga—Lake in the Alagadiço Novo area, about two leagues from the capital. The indigenous name means "red eyes,": from *ceça*, "eyes," and *piranga*, "red." This same name is commonly given in the North to a certain type of opthalmia.

4. Muritiapuá—From *muriti*, the name of the palm commonly known as *buriti*, and *apuã*, "island." A small town at the previously cited location.

5. Aratanha—From *arara*, "bird," and *tanha*, "beak." A highly fertile, cultivated sierra, a continuation of the Maranguape.

6. Guaiúba—From *goaia*, "valley," *y*, "water," *jur*, "to come," and *be*, "through which": through which come the waters of the valley. A river that rises in the Aratanha sierra and cuts through the town of the same name, six leagues from the capital.

7. Pacatuba—From *paca* and *tuba*, "bed or refuge of the cavies." A recent but important town in the beautiful valley of the Aratanha sierra.

8. Ambergris—The beaches of Ceará in those times were very abundant in ambergris tossed up by the sea. The indigenous peoples called it *pira repor*, "fish dung."

XXIV

1. Coatiabo—History mentions the fact of Martim Soares Moreno having painted himself while he lived among the savages of Ceará. *Coatiá* means "to paint." The suffix *abo* signifies the object that received the action of the verb, and without doubt it comes from *aba*, "people, creature."

XXV

1. Hummingbird—Simão de Vasconcelos speaks of this lethargy of the hummingbird in winter.

2. Carbeto—A kind of evening gathering of the Indians in a larger hut where everyone met to talk. See Ives d'Évreux, *Viagem ao Norte do Brasil*.

XXVI

1. Mecejana—A lake and town two leagues from the capital, The verb *cejar* means "to abandon"; the suffix *ana* indicated the person exercising the action of the verb. *Cejana* means "one who abandons." In combination with the particle *mo* from the verb *monhang*, "to do," the word comes to mean "he who made to abandon" or "which was the place and occasion of abandoning." The general opinion is that the name of the town comes from Portugal, like Soure and Arronches. In that case it should be written *Mesejana*, from the Arabic *masjana*.

Now, in older documents one finds *Mecejana*, with a *c*, which would indicate a rather unnatural alteration, when Ceará was populated exclusively by the Portuguese, who preserved in their purity all other names of Portuguese origin.

2. Monguba—A tree that yields a fruit full of down, similar to that of the silk-cotton tree, with the difference that it is dark. From it comes the name of part of the Maranguape range.

XXVII

1. Mombin—Fruit of the Araripe sierra which is not found on the coast. It is tasty and similar to the cashew.

2. Jacarecanga—Hill of sand on the beach of Ceará, famed as a source of the purest cool water. It comes from *jacaré*, "crocodile," and *acanga*, "head."

XXVIII

1. Japim—A gold-colored bird with black scapulars and commonly known by the name of *sofrê*.

2. Dark leaf—The myrtle, which the indigenous peoples called *capixuna*, from *caa*, "branches, foliage," and *pixuna*, "dark." From this comes the figure that Iracema uses to express the sadness that she produces in her husband.

XXIX

1. Tupinambás—A formidable nation and a primitive branch of the great Tupi race. After a heroic resistance, unable to expel the Portuguese from Bahia, they emigrated to Maranhão, where they made an alliance with the French, who were already present in large numbers in that area. The name they

gave themselves means "people related to the Tupis," from *tupi*, *anama*, *aba*.

2. Bay of parrots—This is the bay of *Jericoacoara*, from *jeru*, "parrot," *cua*, "meadow," *coara*, "hole or bosom": bay of the meadow of parrots. It is one of the fine ports of Ceará.

3. Maracatim—Large boat that bore in its prow—*tim*—a *maracá*. The smaller boats or canoes were called *igara*, from *ig*, "water," and *jára*, "master": mistress of the water.

4. Caiçara—From *cai*, "burned wood," and the suffix *çara*, "that which has or is made from": that which is made from burned wood. It was a strong wattle-and-daub stockade.

XXX

1. Moacir—Child of suffering; from *moacy*, "pain," and *ira*, suffix signifying "come from."

2. Nursed upon your soul—"Child" in Tupi is *pitanga*, from *piter*, "to suck," and *anga*, "soul": soul-sucker. Could this be because children attract and delight those who see them? Or because they absorb a part of their parents' soul? Caubi speaks in this latter sense.

XXXI

1. Carimã—A well-known preparation made from manioc. *Caric*, "to run," *mani*, "manioc": drained manioc.

XXXII

1. Tauape—"Place of yellow clay"; from *tauá* and *ipé*. It is on the route to Maranguape.

2. Piau—The fish that gave its name to the Piauí River.

3. Old village—Translation of *Tapui-tapera*. This was what one of the Tupinambá establishments in Maranhão was called.

4. Itaoca—"House of stone," fortress.

5. Manacá—A beautiful flower. Consult what Sr. Gonçalves Dias says about it in his dictionary.

6. Cupim—The familiar termite. The name is composed of *co*, "hole," and *pim*, "barb."

XXXIII

1. Albuquerque—Jerônimo de Albuquerque, leader of the expedition to Maranhão in 1612.

Letter to Dr. Jaguaribe

Here I am again, as promised. You have read the book and the notes that accompany it; so let's talk.

Let's talk without ceremony, with total familiarity, as if each of us were reclining in his hammock, to the sway of the languid rocking that invites one to pleasant conversation.

If some reader cares to listen, let him. Not for that reason shall we exchange the humble tone of intimacy for the elegant phrases of the salon.

To begin.

You must remember a night when, coming into my house, four years ago you found me scribbling a book. This was at an important time, for a new legislature, creature of a new law, was holding its first session, and the country's eyes were turned to it, from which was expected a generous initiative toward a better situation.

I was rather skeptical about things, and more so about men; and that was why I sought in literature diversion from the sadness that the state of a nation benumbed by indifference instilled in me. I thought, however, that you, a politician of older and better temperament, took little interest in things literary, not because of disdain but by vocation.

The conversation that we had then revealed my mistake; I discovered a cultivator and friend of light literature; and together we read some passages from the work, which had—and has not yet lost—pretensions to a poem.

And, as you saw and as I outlined to you in broad strokes, a heroid that has as its subject the traditions of the indigenous peoples of Brazil and their customs. I did not ever recall dedicating myself to that genre of literature, from which I always abstained, once the first and fleeting raptures of youth were past. One can bear mediocre prose, and it is even esteemed by the degree of excellence of its ideas; but mediocre verse is the worst tragedy that can be inflicted on the pious reader.

I committed an imprudence when I wrote some letters about the Tamoio Confederation and said: "The traditions of the indigenous peoples offer material for a great poem that someone may one day present, quietly and without fanfare, as the modest fruit of his sleepless nights."

That was enough for it to be supposed that the writer was referring to himself, and that he already had the poem completed; several people asked me about it. This instilled in me a sense of literary pride; without calculating the minimum effort needed for such a large undertaking, which humbled two illustrious poets, I sketched the design of the work and began with such a vigor that I was able to take it to the fourth canto almost in a single breath.

That breath lasted for about five months, but faded away, and I'll tell you the reason.

From the early stages, when the first literary urges began, an instinct of some kind impelled my imagination toward the indigenous savage race. I say instinct, because at the time I had not done sufficient study to appreciate properly the nationality of a literature; it was simple pleasure that brought me to reading the old chronicles and memoirs.

Later, discerning things better, I read publications about the theme of the indigenous peoples; they did not achieve the national poetry that I found in the savage life of the aboriginal Brazilians. Many of them fell short from their abuse of one indigenous term after another, which not only broke the harmony of the Portuguese language but also distorted the interpretation of the text. Others were exquisite in style and rich in beautiful images; they lacked, however, a certain ingenuous coarseness of thought and expression that should be the speech of indigenous peoples.

Gonçalves Dias is our national poet par excellence; he has no peer in the opulence of his imagination, in the delicate lapidary of his verse, in his knowledge of Brazilian nature and savage customs. In his South American poems he made use of many of the loveliest traditions of the indigenous peoples, and his unfinished poem "Timbiras," he proposed to depict the Brazilian epopee.

Nonetheless, the savages in his poem speak a classical language, for which he was censured by another poet of great creativity, Bernardo Guimarães; they express ideas characteristic of civilized man that lack verisimilitude in the state of nature.

Beyond doubt, the Brazilian poet must translate into his language the Indians' ideas, though they be crude and coarse; but it is in that tradition that the great difficulty lies: it is necessary for the civilized language to mold itself as much as it can to the primitive simplicity of the barbaric tongue and not represent indigenous images and thoughts except by terms and phrases that strike the reader as natural in the mouths of savages.

Knowledge of the indigenous language is the best criterion for the nationalization of literature. It provides us with not only the true style but also the savage's poetic images, his ways of thought, the inclinations of his spirit, and even the smallest details of his life.

It is from that fount that the Brazilian poet should drink: it is from it that the true Brazilian poem, as I imagine, is to come.

Therefore, committing that great act of daring, I took advantage of the desire to realize the ideas that were drifting about in my mind and were not as yet a firm plan: reflection consolidated and strengthened them.

They were poured into the written part of the work in great quantity. If the laborious investigation of native beauties done with imperfect and spurious dictionaries drained the soul, the satisfaction of cultivating these wildflowers of Brazilian poetry brought delight. One day, however, fatigued by continuous and uninterrupted meditation to discover the etymology of a word, I was beset by apprehension.

Would all this arduous labor that a single word sometimes cost me be taken into account? Would it be known that this scruple of fine gold had been mined from the deep layer where an extinct race sleeps? Or would it be thought that it had been found on the surface and had come about through facile inspiration?

And, in regard to that, another immediate misgiving.

Would the image or thought, carefully polished at the cost of so much toil, be appreciated in all its value by the majority of readers? Would they not judge them inferior to the fashionable images used in modern literature?

An example, taken from this book, comes to mind. The indigenous peoples called a guide *piguara*, master of the pathway. The beauty of the savage expression in its literal and etymological translation seems quite salient to me. They did not say "knower," although they had a term of their own, *couab*, because that phrase did not express the force of their thought. In the savage state, a pathway does not exist; it is nothing to be known; it is made on the occasion of the advance across the forest or countryside, and in a certain direction. He who has it and gives it is really master of the pathway.

Isn't that lovely? Isn't there a gem of Brazilian poetry there?

Now, there will be those who prefer the expression "king of the pathway," although the natives of Brazil had neither a king or any idea of such an institution. Others leaned toward the word "guide," as simpler and more natural in Portuguese, though it does not correspond to the savage's thought.

Writing a poem, possibly a long one, to run the risk of not being understood, and if understood not appreciated, was enough to dishearten even the heartiest of talents, much less my own mediocrity. What to do? Fill the book with italics, which would make it more disorderly, and with notes that no one reads? Publish the work partially so that the cognoscenti could offer their literary verdict? Give a reading of it to a select circle that would issue an enlightened judgment?

All these methods had their drawbacks, and all were rejected: the first disfigured the book; the second cut it into pieces; the third would not be advantageous because of the ceremonious benevolence of critics. What seemed best and more judicious was to redirect the spirit of the work and give it a new course.

But a book already begun is not abandoned in such a manner, however bad it may be: there in those pages filled with erasures and inkblots sleeps the larva of the thought, which can be a nymph with golden wings if inspiration fertilizes the coarse cocoon. In the divers pauses of its preoccupation, my spirit would return to the book where close to two thousand lines of heroic poetry already are, and will be, incubated.

Depending on the benevolence or severity of my conscience, I sometimes find them pretty and worthy of seeing the light of day; at other times they strike me as vulgar, monotonous, and inferior to much of the coarse prose that I have laid out on paper. If, after all, a father's love assuages this rigor, it still never dispels the fear of "wasting my time writing useless verses for backwoodsmen."

On one of my spirit's returns to the already-begun work, I remembered to try an experiment in prose. Verse, because of its dignity and nobility, does not admit of a certain flexibility of expression that nevertheless is not unbecoming to the most elevated prose. The elasticity of the sentence would thus permit the indigenous phrases to be utilized with greater clarity so that they would not go unnoticed. On the other hand, the intended effect of the verse would become known by the effect of the prose.

The subject for the experiment was already found. When I again saw our native land in 1848, I had the idea of using its legends and traditions in a literary work. In São Paulo, I had already begun a biography of Camarão. His youth, the heroic friendship that joined him to Soares Moreno, the courage and loyalty of Jacaúna, ally of the Portuguese, and his wars against the celebrated Round-Honey: there was the theme. It lacked the perfume that a woman's soul effuses in the passions of a man.

Now you know my other reason for directing the book to you; I needed to say all these things, tell how and why I wrote *Iracema*. And who better with whom to converse about this than a witness to my work, the only one of the few who now breathe the zephyrs of Ceará?

This book is therefore an experiment, or rather an exhibit. You will find realized in it my ideas about Brazilian literature, and you will find there poetry entirely Brazilian, absorbed from the language of the savages. The etymology of the names of the several locales, as well as certain figures of speech taken from the composition of words, are coinages.

Understand that I could not spread these riches abundantly through the modest book now published, for they would have been despoiled in a work of greater bulk, which would have only the novelty of fable. There is, however, more than enough there to provide material for criticism and serve as basis for judgment by the cognoscenti.

If the reading public likes this literary form, which appears to me to have some attraction, then an effort will be made to finish the poem that has been started, although the verse has lost much of its primitive enchantment. If, however, the book is censured as trite, and *Iracema* encounters the customary indifference that greets both the good and the bad with the same complacency, when not with disdainful and ungrateful silence; in that case the author will despair of this genre of literature also, as he has despaired of theater, and the verses, like the plays will go into the drawer for old papers, mere autobiographical relics.

After the book was finished, and when I reread it polished and already in press, I saw shortcomings that had escaped my attention and must be corrected: I note some excess of comparisons, the repetition of certain images, stylistic lapses in the final chapters. It also seems to me that I should preserve names of localities in their present, albeit corrupted, forms.

If the work has a second edition, it will be purged of these and other defects that the cognoscenti may uncover.

J. de Alencar
August, 1865

Afterword

Iracema: **Poetry and Colonization**

by Alcides Villaça

Over the course of time, *Iracema* has been categorized by critics as an Indianist novel, Brazilian legend, prose poem, romantic epic, American fantasy, Tupi Indian pastoral, Romanesque myth, and lyrical novel, among many others. The difficulty in critically pinning down the exact genre of a work never makes much difference in a reader's spontaneous pleasure, but, later on, it might prompt the reader to reflect on the peculiar qualities of the text that captivated him or her. The many different reading perspectives implied by those designations do justice to the involuntary complexity of the work. Yes, involuntary: Alencar conceived it in a single-minded way; he baptised it "Legend of Ceará," inscribing it in the field of fantasy fed by a historical plot. It so happens that precisely this project—to set free fantasy against a backdrop inspired by history—works on a delicate axis of antagonistic forces.

Iracema is the poetic reconciliation of several mutually opposing forces. Reading the work with lyrical involvement does not rule out the interest it holds as an expression of ideology: this dual perspective allows us to take in fully the field of forces in which it functions. When history, poetry, and ideology come together and fuse, the different levels of value commingle in the complex unity of the final artistic effect.

Style and Impressions

When we come to the end of *Iracema*, what impressions stay with us? Most likely they will not be those arising from the complexity of the plot, from the clear-cut psychology of the characters, from the construction of a well-marked fictional time. Rather the strength of this work asserts itself, more than anywhere else, in the poetic nature of images and rhythms, in drawing the reader in through the sensitive quality of the words, the phrases, the melodious cadences, the imaginative figures, the subtle hints concentrated in certain key symbols. This means that the effectively narrated story reverberates in a poetic way within readers, drawing them into a double movement: even if they start out by following a more objective and straightforward succession of facts, later they will pause to linger over some special felicity in the novel's language; an exotic word, a deft rhetorical move, a sentimental reflection. The fusion of the fictional and poetic levels is in no way alien to romantic writing, which seeks to break free of the constraints of prescribed genres and lays itself open to the expression of great idealized totalities, such as the commingling of history with legend, with subjective, inner states, with the world of nature, with the epic and lyrical modes. Let us recall the novel's opening lines:

> Green, impetuous seas of my native land, where
> the *jandaia* sings amid the carnauba fronds:
> Green seas, that gleam with liquid emerald in
> the rays of the rising sun, skirting alabaster beaches
> shaded by coconut trees:
> Be still, green seas, and softly caress the raging wave
> so the intrepid boat may calmly float above the waters.

Where is the brave raft bound, rapidly leaving
behind the coast of Ceará, with its great sail open
to the cool wind from the shore?
Where is it bound, like a white kingfisher seek-
ing the native cliff in the ocean's solitude?

The rhetorical expressions—"liquid emerald," "skirting
alabaster beaches shaded by coconut trees," "cool wind from
the shore," "native cliff"—and the repeated invocation of
"green seas" have the ring of epic poetry. Alencar incorpo-
rates, nonetheless, local, particular elements (*jandaia, car-
naúba, jangada, raft, Ceará*) that, without lowering the tone,
begin to sketch in the landscape of "my native land," as the
narrator says, speaking in his own voice. The rustic *jangada*
(raft) is compared with the "white kingfisher," a bird from
classical antiquity; such a comparison, far from being unin-
tentional, announces the structural method employed in
Iracema: the constant use of similes, which will function in a
skillful system of translations. In effect, the narrator is posi-
tioning himself as a resolute mediator between the oppos-
ing realities and cultures that will be represented in the
figures of Iracema and Martim. Striving for a fully empa-
thetic view of both, he is getting ready to follow them as
they come together and move apart, and to observe the var-
ious aspects of their subjective, social, and ethnic features.

Alencar then grew apprehensive over the difficulty of
the task. He realized intuitively that poetic fidelity to the
heroine and her people implied making at least some ges-
ture toward the language of that culture, where its distinc-
tive way of describing and understanding the world is
formulated. He chose to have continual recourse to similes
and epithets, in the Homeric manner, so that a name (such
as *Iracema*) would be immediately translated to its literal
meaning (*honey lips*). In this way, the story of Iracema is
presented to us through the elegance of a refined Por-
tuguese that incorporates, or alludes poetically to, the Tupi
language's resources of construction and expression.

Civilization and Destiny

Readers will recall that, up to a certain point in the novel
(let's call it a novel, to keep things simple), Martim is un-
der the brave and watchful protection of Iracema and,
through her intermediation, that of Araquém, Andira,
and Caubi, against the hostility of Chief Irapuã and his
warriors; and it will also be remembered that from the
middle to the end of the novel all the initiative passes to
Martim, who, together with his Pitiguara allies, goes to
battle to conquer the Tabajaras. From this point on,
Iracema is always the one who follows her beloved white
warrior, carrying the burden of having surrendered, along
with her body, the "secret of the *jurema* tree," and of hav-
ing allied herself with Martim to defeat her own people.
The fact that she willfully takes in Martim, and her deter-
mined resignation in the face of destiny, tell us a good deal
about Alencar's implicit conception of colonial history.
Iracema's generous nature translates into hospitality and
the sacrificial passion of one who warmly welcomes and
submits—a broader simile for a beautiful and virtuous
nature surrendering to the invincible onslaught of civiliza-
tion. First the active and later the passive mate of Martim,
the Indian heroine renounces her Tabajara identity to ac-
company the restless warrior on his colonizing missions.
This renunciation would be an act of unacceptable treach-
ery, were there not an overriding force to justify it, via a
sublimating strategy the author has created: Iracema is in
thrall, even more than to her native identity, to the ro-
mantic, idealizing conception of Woman; more than be-
ing guided by customs deeply rooted in tribal culture,
Iracema allows herself to be possessed by the tragic force
of romantic love. The dramatic character of the Indian
heroine arises from the conflict represented by the forced
choice between two renunciations: either renouncing the
commitments she has because of her origin, commitments
to the tribal order, or renouncing the truth of love.

Within this system of ideas, readers will observe that the poetic innocence that gives the novel its tone is not unaffected by the historical forces that make up its backdrop. Iracema's resigned attitude inevitably ties into a resigned nature, which already has come to include the culture of a primitive people lacking means of resistance in the face of a well-armed colonizer. While Iracema's first impulse is to put an arrow through the unknown warrior (Chapter II), her second is to take pity on him, take him in, and give herself to him.

In seeking to understand the project behind Alencar's novel, one should note that his nationalism has no trace of antipathy toward the colonizer, a progressive warrior whom the novel praises for his energy; nor does it dismiss the poetry of virgin nature and the "natural" virtues of the natives, virtues sung from Montaigne to Rousseau. It is a matter, then, of not betraying nationalistic ideals—either in their mythic foundations, which uphold them symbolically, or in their mission of building up and civilizing the country, which constructs the future. Sublimation appears inevitable; the ideology of progress has long been the mortal enemy of any type of mythology, and this contradiction certainly did not appear as such to Alencar's eyes. What we are given, then, is a celebration of sublime resignation as a natural virtue, ascribed to the Indian woman in particular and woman in general, even if they end up sacrificed to the constructive mission—equally virtuous—of the white male warrior. It's true that the narrator is sympathetically inclined toward the heroine, to whose intimate world he attributes the utmost delicacy and sensitivity, imbuing her with a poetic integrity that enhances her in the reader's eyes; however, it is also true that the grief and death of the Indian heroine come about as the result of a cruel fate set in motion entirely by the presence of the colonizer. The reproaches that could potentially be leveled against Martim for his insensitivity toward, neglect of, and wavering attachment to Iracema seem to have been warded off in advance

by the narrator's zealous reminders that the warrior is dedi-
cated to carrying out the highest mission. Significantly,
Iracema understands from the very start that her lover's
eyes and heart "are far away," and belong to another story.
Even as she nurtures an intense love for Martim, she recog-
nizes that it is incompatible with her lover's destiny when
she tells him "The honey of Iracema's lips is like the honey-
comb that the bees make in the *andiroba* trunk: there is poi-
son in its sweetness. The blue-eyed maiden with hair the
color of the sun keeps for her warrior in the white man's vil-
lage the honey of the white lily."

The opposing forces that the Indian heroine is ponder-
ing here correspond exactly to the intimate desires and
thoughts of Martim, who, at another point in the story,
rocking in the hammock, feels that "There, the blonde
maiden awaited him with her chaste affection; here, the
dark maiden smiled at him with her ardent love." Alencar
could not have found a more apt expression to set out
with such perfect symmetry the two poles of a historical
and amorous dilemma frequently found in romanticism.

Love and Nature

In Indianist literature, the romantic writer enjoys the op-
tion of taking a certain liberty, which he or she often ex-
ercises to great advantage: the possibility of rising above
the conflict between eroticism and idealism. This conflict
can be very thorny when it involves the white virgin, who
is almost always elevated to the heights of clouds, the
moon, and the stars, until she can scarcely receive the
lightest touch of a vague sensuality. The Indian woman
already inherently bears the mark of nature's innocence,
which will by no means be compromised if she enters
into a love affair. So, through constant reminders of this
natural setting, of which she is the mirror and to which
she is an intimate link, the native lover frees the romantic
lover from the scruples that, back in society, would lead

him into matrimony and domesticity: a prosaic solution with which, understandably, many stories must end (including *Senhora*, another of Alencar's novels). The Indian mistress offers the pleasure of immediate, ardent passion, directly linked to the forces of nature and for that very reason rendered sublime. (In the work of the romantic poet Antônio Gonçalves Dias as well, particularly in his beautiful poem "Bed of Green Leaves," one finds the compelling spontaneity of an Indian woman recalling her first lover, as she gives herself over to the voluptuous anticipation of an amorous encounter, in the midst of a spectacularly sensual nature.)

The sense of sin cannot be associated with Iracema, because in nature there is neither guilt nor forgiveness. Yet, shouldn't it threaten to tarnish the reputation of Martim, who is so often referred to emphatically as "the Christian"? Alencar was diligent in his efforts to keep his hero's honor from being sullied; afflicted with scruples, Martim resists his first moments of temptation to possess the Indian maiden, warding off her advances with the invocation "Christ! . . . Christ! . . ." Then, kept awake by the torments of desire, he is ensnared by the bitter green liquor of Tupã; after drinking it, "he could be with Iracema and gather from her lips the kisses that luxuriated there among the smiles, like fruit in the flower's corolla. He could love her and imbibe the honey and perfume from that love without leaving poison in the maiden's breast." The stratagem employed here is just as malicious as it would be—from Alencar's point of view—for Martim to commit the sin in cold blood. Nor can it go unnoticed that, in this passage, amorous possession is associated with the availability of that "fruit in the flower's corolla," which seems to offer itself up so seductively and naturally. Strictly speaking, "the Christian" commits the act in his sleep, while unconscious; yet he nevertheless enjoys complete physical pleasure and release. Once again the narrative ascribes to the white warrior a carefully justified and fruitful impulse, while it assigns to Iracema the poetic task of dealing with the consequences with all her courage, nobility, and sublimity. Symbolically, at this moment she is abandoned by nature, which up to then has been hers. Ara, the *jandaia* bird who has been her sister and friend, takes flight, "never to return to the hut." It now falls Iracema's lot to fulfill, in intimate solitude, a destiny that was not originally hers. In accepting it, she rises in stature as a heroine in the eyes of the narrator; her faithfulness to Martim complies both with an ethical system in which Indians appear as figures of loyalty, and the precept of Christian marriage summarized in "for richer or for poorer, in sickness and in health, as long as ye both shall live." Iracema follows this dictum—only to suffer, conceive, give birth to a mestizo son, and die.

Magic and Desacralization

One episode in particular is revealing in depicting reconciliation between opposing forces. When Araquém, as pajé of the Tabajaras, invokes the power of thunder, lo and behold, a thunderous roar is heard when he picks up a stone from the ground: "From the deep cavern came a frightful moan that seemed to be torn from the rock's very entrails." This becomes a very persuasive weapon to protect the white warrior. At first, the voice of that divine fury will sound as strange to the reader as it seemed to Martim. The Christian warrior's doubt is associated with the reader's incredulity: "he could not believe that the god of the Tabajaras had given his priest so much power." But Alencar will explain later that, in fact, no god would turn Araquém into such a portentous figure; the "voice of Tupã" was the echo of the sea waves pounding on the rocks, bouncing off the walls of an underground chamber where the pajé had, providentially, built his hut. When the stone was removed, the opening let out the "frightful moan."

The episode illustrates the caution with which Alencar treated the pagan version of a miracle, which is duly debunked by the laws of physics. But there is more to it: the outsider becomes privy to the true source of the pajé's "power," so that then both of them are in together on the secret of the deception required to keep the credulous warriors terrified. The same "sacred" underground chamber—supposedly Tupã's throat—will later become Martim's escape route. Colonization implies, among so many other consequences, the desacralization of the colonized culture; in this episode, the virtue of primitive magic is mixed together with the display of a power that belongs to nature and for which a natural explanation can be given with pragmatic simplicity.

The Poetry of Iracema

It would be unfair to the novel to do nothing but point out the distortions of an ideology that was widespread at the time and was embraced by the author. *Iracema*, as we stated at the outset, achieves true poetic triumphs, which create an unforgettable image of the heroine. It is, to be sure, not the image of a historical Indian woman, since we have entered what Antônio Cândido has called "fantasized ethnography." Rather it is an image of a "natural" woman, a myth and a figure emblematic of primitively beautiful nature. Iracema acts upon intuitions that accurately reflect the force of destiny, and she expresses herself in a language that can stand as lyrical and tragic poetry. Instinctive on the one hand, yet on the other reflective, the heroine bears the melancholy shadow of one who is living out her death. Living amidst nature, she is consoled by it and expresses through it her innermost experiences: her awareness and feelings immediately assume concrete form through similes, so that everything occurring in her interior reality has its equivalent projection in the natural world.

By means of Iracema, the reader feels vividly the mythic conviction that all the world is the expression of a greater truth, which reveals itself to the senses through nature: the passion flower incarnates the power of memory, the oyster clinging to the rocks invokes constancy; the sea breeze rippling through the leaves is sweet nothings; the waxing and waning melancholy of the characters is marked by the flowering of the cashew; worktime is indicated by the *sabiá* birds falling silent. Place names tell the tale of deeds, mark the passage of human beings, and suggest moods; words and expressions have their roots in physical nature, humanizing it. Personal names can both speak of the past and be prophetic: from Iracema and Martim is born Moacir, the child of suffering. The mestizo whose arrival is announced here will live out a history in which times of resignation will alternate with moments of resistance. He will be the mulatto overseer, the bandit, the sharecropper, the outlaw, the tenement-dweller, the migrant fleeing drought-stricken regions, the soldier, the fanatic, the worker, the petty bureaucrat— and, in these various incarnations, he will appear as the main character of several masterpieces of Brazilian literature.

At the end of the book, Alencar brings to fulfillment the poetic design of his Iracema, identifying her with the coconut palm beneath which she has been buried: the Indian heroine is set down for all time as the image of pure nature, becoming the greatest symbol of historical-nationalistic romanticism and of Brazilian lyricism.

Let there stand, as a final note, the suggestive power of the last phrase of the novel: "On earth, all things pass away." In the immediate context, it refers to the oblivion that swallows up Iracema's name when the *jandaia* bird ceases to sing it, and the fleetingness of the things of this world. It is difficult, however, not to take it also as a pessimistic shadowing boding ill—that even in his confident nationalism, Alencar cast over the future of the myths and poetry of peoples and communities.